D1225627

CREATION REBORN

CREATION REBORN

YOUR INVITATION TO GOD'S DIVINE DESIGN

ABNER SUAREZ

Creation Reborn - Your Invitation to God's Divine Design

Copyright © 2014 – Abner Suarez

All rights reserved. This book is protected by the copyright laws of the United States of America. No part of this publication may be reproduced, stored in a retrieval system or transmitted in any form or by any means – electronic, mechanical, photocopy, recording or any other – except for brief quotations, without the prior permission of the author.

Unless otherwise noted, Scripture is taken from the New King James Version of the Bible®. Copyright ©1982 by Thomas Nelson, Inc. Used by permission. All rights reserved.

Scripture quotations marked NIV are taken from THE HOLY BIBLE, NEW INTERNATIONAL VERSION®, NIV® Copyright © 1973, 1978, 1984, 2011 by Biblica, Inc.® Used by permission. All rights reserved worldwide.

Scripture marked ESV is taken from The Holy Bible, English Standard Version® (ESV®), copyright © 2001 by Crossway, a publishing ministry of Good News Publishers. Used by permission. All rights reserved.

Published by XP Publishing

A department of XPMinistries
P.O. Box 1017
Maricopa, Arizona 85139
Unites States of America
www.XPpublishing.com

ISBN: 978-1-939183-50-7

Printed in the United States of America
For Worldwide Distribution

Distribution by Higher Life - www.ahigherlife.com

ENDORSEMENTS

Abner Suarez is an amazing minister of the gospel who regularly sees the power of God produce healing in his meetings. His new book, *Creation Reborn*, covers many of the priorities that appear to be on God's heart. The book balances the emphases of intimacy and mission. It also emphasizes the importance of hearing from the Lord, obeying the Lord, and speaking out on behalf of the Lord. Loving, worshiping, and obeying God are all addressed. The relationship between declarations of faith and signs, wonders, miracles, and healing is also addressed. I recommend Abner to you as a man after God's heart. I recommend his ministry and his book.

DR. RANDY CLARK
FOUNDER AND PRESIDENT OF
GLOBAL AWAKENING AND THE APOSTOLIC
NETWORK OF GLOBAL AWAKENING
MECHANICSBURG, PENNSYLVANIA
GLOBALAWAKENING.COM

A prophet's job is to see heaven's plans and then proclaim them to the Body of Christ, so that what is being revealed can be accessed and obtained. When God purposed to build a tabernacle in the wilderness, He took Moses onto a high mountain and showed him heavenly visions so that he could, "make them after the pattern for them, which was shown to [him] on the mountain" (Exodus 25:40).

Abner's book, *Creation Reborn: Your Invitation to God's Divine Design*, is a pattern being set forth for a future that is waiting to happen. God's plans are good plans, and Abner is giving us a glimpse into them so that they can manifest in the earth. I found myself being absorbed into the book and caught up with expectation for the days that are coming.

Read this book, get a vision for the years to come, and rise up into the call that is being sounded forth. You won't be disappointed!

JEFF STRUSS

SENIOR LEADER

THE REVIVAL SCENE COMMUNITY CHURCHES

THE LYNCHBURG HOUSE OF PRAYER

WWW.THEREVIVALSCENE.COM

Abner Suarez, through his book *Creation Reborn*, invites you to partner with God, to walk with God, and to minister through God as He unfolds and establishes His eternal plans and purposes for these days through His church. He invites you to dream big as you see God's glory in this hour fill the earth as it never has before in all of mankind's history. God does not want to accomplish this without YOU. I love this! Brilliant!

PATRICIA KING

FOUNDER OF XP MINISTRIES

WWW.XPMINISTRIES.COM

In Abner's book, *Creation Reborn*, we see the possibilities of God. *Creation Reborn* shows us what a sanctified imagination can see. This book brought me to tears on several occasions. Abner paints a picture of the transformation of people and the reformation of a city. He also gives us detailed biblical insight into how we can get there. This book will strengthen your love for Jesus, build your faith in Jesus and fill you with hope for the world. Let this book inspire you to let Christ shine through you.

ADAM LIVECCHI
FOUNDER OF WE SEE JESUS MINISTRIES AND
AUTHOR OF GO.PREACH.HEAL
WWW.WESEEJESUSMINISTRIES.COM

We are living in historic and very trying times of the last days described by the apostle Paul in 2 Timothy 3:1-5. In this eye-opening book, Abner, through an exciting story and teaching, gives us revelatory insight into the role of the Church and how we, as disciples of Christ, are to live and achieve victory for the Kingdom of God. This is a must-read for every serious Christian!!!

DR. JAMES A. BRICE, JR., SR. PASTOR,
COVENANT LOVE CHURCH, FAYETTEVILLE, NC
WWW.COVENANTLOVECHURCH.ORG

Jesus said in Luke 17:21, "For behold the Kingdom of God is in the midst of you!" (ESV) That is the exact profound message of Prophet Abner Suarez's book, *Creation Reborn*. I know the heart of the author and I know that this message has burned in his spirit for years. Get ready to be taken on a journey of a lifetime as you begin to realize that God's DNA is in you. This book is for every believer who is desperate to understand the heart of God for his people. I believe that this book will become an instant classic in the long line of books written at critical moments in history as a blueprint for next-level Christians. I must tell you that if you truly heed this message your world and the world around you will never be the same. Let's change the world, before the world changes us! Rise up church!"

Patrick Schatzline, Evangelist,
Mercy Seat Ministries
Author of "Why is God so mad at me"
and "I am Remnant!"
www.mercyseatministries.com

Abner has given the reader a strong biblical foundation for all true believers to build upon. I especially enjoyed following the Robinson family through their transformation from a normal, lukewarm Christian family into a powerfully anointed team who has learned to hear the voice of God and then to follow where He leads and being amazed by how God uses them in the work of His Kingdom. I WAS READY TO JOIN THEM IN THOSE AWESOME MEETINGS AT NOTRE DAME STADIUM IN SOUTH BEND BUT THEN REALIZED THEY HAVEN'T HAPPENED YET.

Apostle John Ross
Cloud 9 Worship Center
Spring Valley, California
www.cloud9wc.org

Creation Reborn is a practical, inspirational and informative tool to guide you into a revolutionary shift personally and globally. Your eyes will be opened to God's big picture, God's dream. As you read *Creation Reborn* you will experience the Father's tug on your heart to be a part of His dream team as you become who He has designed you to be and shift you into what He has designed you to do. Welcome to God's divine design.

TRACEY ARMSTRONG
FOUNDER, CITADEL CHURCHES
BEST SELLING AUTHOR OF "FOLLOWERSHIP"
WWW.TRACEYARMSTRONG.COM

You can't help but notice a credibility gap between what's preached and what's demonstrated in the American Church today. Thankfully, God noticed too and has raised up prophetic voices to shrink the gap and restore the Church to its New Testament glory. I am happy to say Abner Suarez is one these voices. I believe this book is a gift to the body of Christ to stir the hearts of believers who want to be used by the Holy Spirit in this present day.

JARED RUDDY
SENIOR LEADER CITY LIGHTS CHURCH
SCRANTON, PENNYSLVANIA
CITYLIGHTSCHURCH.NET

DEDICATION

To my parents Angel and Sara Suarez, who provided the incredible foundation for me to step into the purpose of God all the days of my life.

I am so thankful that our heavenly Father gave me the honor to be called your son. You have established a Godly heritage for Angie, Leo, and me, and by God's grace I hope to accelerate in the coming years. Thanks does not seem sufficient, but *thank you*!

ACKNOWLEDGMENTS

There were countless individuals and churches who prayed, prophesied, and encouraged me in helping making this project a reality; thank you for your encouragement!

In particular I would like to thank the board of For Such A Time As This, Inc, who have stood with me as gatekeepers and spiritual mothers and fathers in my life: Dale and LuAnne Mast, Mike and Debbie Sirianni, Doug & Betsy Johnson, and Grant Berry.

I am also forever indebted to Patrick H. Schatzline for being the first to acknowledge the call of God on my life and for opening the first doors to make that calling a reality.

Finally, a very special thank-you to Dom Crincoli of Crincoli Communications as the first editor on this project. Dom, you took to working this project as if it were your very own, and for that I am forever grateful.

TABLE OF CONTENTS

FOREWORD

Abner's life is marked by an abiding intimacy with God. This book will surely challenge you, even as it provides keys to the pursuit of a deeper spiritual journey. "What we treasure most will command our attention." This is one of many statements from the book that will challenge us in a simple but profound way. *Creation Reborn* will serve as a roadmap and valued resource if you desire a life of increasing intimacy and deep encounters with God. Moses fell before a burning bush. Jacob saw a ladder from heaven. No believer shifts earth without a God-encounter from Heaven. Now it's your turn! - Dale

Abner was used by God to move me forward into my destiny with accurate prophetic insight. There is a strong anointing on his life to teach and release the fire and glory of God. He is in my book, "God, I Feel Like Cinderella!" - LuAnne

Dale and LuAnne Mast
Pastors of Destiny Christian Church
Eagle Fire Ministries
Dover, Delaware

CREATION REBORN IS YOUR INVITATION TO DREAM
OF SEEING EVERY IMPOSSIBILITY BOW TO THE
KINGDOM OF GOD.

WAS THAT GOD?
OR WAS IT SIMPLY MY IMAGINATION GONE WILD?

What I saw was too brilliant to be my imagination. While beginning my day with a time of devotion, I was taken by a vision. In this vision I saw a stadium filled with a shimmering mist that I sensed was the tangible glory of the Lord. From the mist I saw a body being raised from the dead. As my view panned out I could see God's presence was not only visiting the stadium but an entire city. The presence was so wonderfully beautiful and powerful. Through this divine encounter, God was giving me a vision of the future as He intended.

We live in a time when God is stirring the church. His intention is to make all believers active participants in His divine plans by giving them a vision of the future – a future they will help to shape.

Creation Reborn not only gives you a glimpse into a future that's possible, it offers practical principles on how you can begin to live into this heavenly future. I should warn you that if we as a people are going to be obedient to God's purposes in this hour, we are entering uncharted territory. Just as Peter followed Jesus' invitation to walk on water, we too are being invited to walk on water and advance the Kingdom of God into places previous generations never dreamed of.

Creation Reborn is your invitation to dream of seeing every impossibility bow to the Kingdom of God. The foundation of a reformed life is that we be wholly given to friendship with God. This book invites you to build your life on the foundation of a profound relationship with God. Know this: Friendship with God always results in supernatural encounters. It is your invitation to a supernatural life of deep encounters with God.

The message you will find in this book has been birthed from the fruit of walking with the Father for more than eighteen years. As I have been faithful to share this message, I have seen the lives of individuals, church leaders, and networks of churches changed forever through a wonderful outpouring of the Holy Spirit. *Creation Reborn* may help you redefine what we in the Western world consider normal Christianity. I understand that not everyone is hungry for more of God, for more intimacy, and supernatural encounters. I hope you are one who is eager to experience more.

Each chapter of this book begins with a fictional story of John and Diana Robinson. My prayer is that reading their story gives you a small prophetic picture of what I believe to be the heart of God. Our ability to imagine what is possible in the world we live in is crucial to our partnership with the Father in the season of reformation that is upon us. My prayer is that as you read this account, your own imagination will soar with heaven's heartbeat of what is possible for your life, your family, and in the part of the world in which you live.

While the story is a fictional narrative, the encounters, miracles, and prophecies found in the story are real. They are part of my own personal journey with the Father. As you read this account may you find yourself stirred to draw nearer to the Father and to experience the majesty and beauty of God in a way you have not known.

This book is a clarion call to be part of movement that God has inaugurated to reshape the world. It has been the desire of His heart since the beginning of time and has been birthed for such a time as this! May you be one of many who are known as reformers for the day and time in which you live!

THE PRINCIPLES IN THIS BOOK ARE KEYS THAT WILL PROVIDE A WINESKIN OF UNDERSTANDING THAT WILL SUSTAIN THE PEOPLE OF GOD DURING THE COMING OUTPOURING OF THE HOLY SPIRIT, THE LIKES OF WHICH THE WORLD HAS NEVER SEEN.

CHAPTER ONE

GOD'S PLAN FOR PLANET EARTH

It's 6:30 p.m. at John and Diana Robinson's home in South Bend, Indiana. Diana is preparing dinner for her family of five after a long day of work. She's also helping her children with their homework assignments—assignments they *claimed* were already completed.

Cable news blares in the kitchen as she seasons the meat and simmers the vegetables. Suddenly the anchor begins describing unusual occurrences taking place in the South Bend area, interviewing people who tell of dramatic personal encounters with the Person of Jesus Christ. Some say Jesus appeared to them personally, while others describe visions or dreams, rapturous trips to heaven and other life-changing encounters. An invasion of God has overtaken the city of South Bend.

The encounters take place everywhere: in restaurants, schools and universities, at town halls, malls, and financial centers. Life has come to a standstill in many areas as people gather to worship and adore the Person of Jesus Christ. Reporters covering these events seem mystified and troubled. One reporter takes his camera crew to one of these spontaneous gatherings in front of Notre Dame Stadium where a young interviewee explains: "I've found a reason to live and I want to spend the rest of my life worshipping the One who gave me life." An older man echoes the sentiment: "Forty years ago the Holy Spirit promised me that I would live to see the greatest outpouring the world has ever seen, and I believe it has begun."

AN INVASION OF GOD HAS OVERTAKEN

THE CITY OF SOUTH BEND.

The reporter wraps up his interviews and turns things back to the anchor, who is broadcasting from New York. But there's a problem. The anchor is in tears and trembles under the presence of God on national television. He tells the audience he's never felt anything like what he's experiencing. Embarrassed, the news producers cut to a commercial, but not before the well-known atheist stares into the camera and blurts: "This is really God. If this is from heaven, I want to go to there!"

Diana, riveted to the television, realizes an hour has passed and she's made little headway on the meal. She then realizes a pain she's had in her neck for the last fifteen years has disappeared. She looks at her three children, ages seven through fourteen, who usually can't stand watching cable news—or anything else she and her husband enjoy watching—and they too are glued to the TV reports. It's as though the power of an unseen world has come to earth.

Diana and her husband adjust to the "new normal" during the following weeks. The public school where Diana has taught for five years becomes a place of divine encounter—a place to meet with God. As she pulls into the teachers' parking lot in the morning, it's not uncommon now to see colleagues so filled and overcome with the presence of God that they have trouble emerging from their cars. Routine school assemblies normally scheduled for forty-five minutes now go on for three or four hours as students break out in spontaneous praise to God. Many of Diana's most challenging students have been transformed into her finest, and those struggling with learning disabilities are beginning to learn at levels previously thought impossible.

"Church life" in the city of South Bend has been radically altered. New converts enter the Kingdom by the thousands every day. Most churches can't contain the crowds. Some meet every day of the week, while others offer multiple services or join in city-wide meetings at Notre Dame Stadium and the Joyce Center. It is often difficult to teach or preach at the stadium gatherings because of the strong, abiding presence of God. The South Bend fire department appeared at one gathering after several sightings of fire were reported—confusing the visible and manifest presence of God with a natural conflagration.

Reporters converge on South Bend en masse to report on what's taking place.

Not every denomination or stream embraces all that God is doing, but general and widespread rejoicing sweeps across the city. Violence and crime have been cut by thirty percent, and some corrupt city leaders publicly confess to deceit and wrongdoing and promise full restitution. Hospitals report an increase in wellness, with a forty-five percent reduction in their number of patients. The economically depressed downtown area seems to be coming alive with new business ventures and entrepreneurial activity. Apparently, the move of the Holy Spirit is influencing every sphere of society.

A UNIQUE MOMENT IN HUMAN HISTORY

We live in a time when God is fulfilling His plans for Planet Earth. He has chosen us to be a part of His plan for the greatest outpouring the world has ever seen. In the fullness of time, God sent His only begotten Son to ransom captive humanity. In the same way, God has pre-ordained this hour for the Church to change the course of world history.

In Matthew 3:2 Jesus commands that we "repent, for the Kingdom is at hand." The word "repentance" that Jesus used is the Greek word *metanoia*, which means a "change of the mind." Jesus further declared that He, not any other man, would build His Church. If we want to enter into all that God has planned for this season, we must embrace a change mindset. As we do so, aligning with His purposes, He will build His Church like we have never seen.

Martin Luther had no intention of sparking reformation when he nailed his Ninety-Five Theses to the door of Wittenberg Castle in Germany on October 31, 1517. But that's exactly what happened. Luther embraced a shift in mindset that caused millions of Christians to root themselves in a biblical standard—*Sola Scriptura*. The Church and the world have never been the same.

Jesus declared that when the Holy Spirit comes upon His people they would be guided into all truth (John 16:13). Heaven's truth will cause us to change the way we think and build His Church. This is an hour of divine positioning, where the Holy Spirit is releasing simple keys to shift us, so that we may inherit the greatest outpouring in the history of the earth. Simple obedience to God's divine pattern will open heaven's door to God's unlimited resources.

Today heaven is releasing a divine pattern—a pattern based on the foundation of Scripture and the rhema word. God is raising up men and women like Luther to align with His divine pattern across the earth. As these men and women embrace a different mindset than the majority of believers, they will encounter resistance from the established churches, just as Luther did in his day.

Heaven's great desire is for the Church to fulfill its true potential, fully and faithfully displaying the Kingdom of God. To illustrate,

THIS IS AN HOUR OF DIVINE POSITIONING, WHERE THE HOLY SPIRIT IS RELEASING SIMPLE KEYS TO SHIFT US, SO THAT WE MAY INHERIT THE GREATEST OUTPOURING IN THE HISTORY OF THE EARTH.

let's say it is time for your family's annual cross-country road trip. Your family has two choices for transportation: a brand new mini-van with all the latest features, or a twenty-year-old vehicle that is leaking oil, has faulty brakes, and needs a new transmission. Option number one should be the logical choice, but let's say some family members want to take the older vehicle for sentimental reasons. While the older vehicle may get you to your destination, it would be an unwise option. In choosing the newer vehicle, your family is not saying that the old one was never useful, but the new vehicle is a better option to get them to their desired destination.

Similarly, in our day the Holy Spirit has offered us a choice. We can embrace the process of Church transformation, or we can choose to stay on the path that we are on even though it will ultimately be much less effective. This will be a choice between "doing OK" and inheriting God's very best. Choosing to drive the new car will be difficult for some, especially many leaders, because the old vehicle still functions at some level. But embracing change is essential. God wants us to use the best resources available so the whole earth can be filled with the knowledge of His glory.

Often what we see in the Church around the world does not reflect what we find in Scripture. The Father's intent is for the gospel of the Kingdom to shape the history of regions, cities and nations. The primitive Church was birthed through the outpouring of the Holy Spirit, as the gift of tongues was given and after Peter's simple gospel message was preached and three thousand souls come into the Kingdom (Acts 2). Luke records that when the gospel was preached in Samaria, great joy came to the city (Acts 8:8). The universal Church is in need of a new reformation.

Reformation is birthed when a man or woman stands in faith and believes God for a scriptural expression—a return to biblical standards not currently modeled by the Christian community as a whole. God is stirring a holy dissatisfaction in the hearts of men and women throughout the earth—dissatisfaction with the current experience of how we represent God on the earth. An essential element of our faith is that it can be seen when exercised properly (James 2:14).

God will find a group of reformers willing to change the course of Church history through simple obedience. This generation of reformers will become stewards of the greatest move of God in world history—not simply an awakening, but a transformation of the planet. It will take great boldness and courage to agree with heaven in this hour. It may cost the lives of some believers, but this is the honor so richly deserved by the God-Man, Jesus Christ.

Throughout Scripture, when the people of God moved in obedience to God's ordained pattern, heaven gave witness and God released His presence in a tangible way. For example, God spoke to Moses in Exodus 25:8-9:

> And let them make Me a sanctuary, that I may dwell among them. According to all that I show you, that is, the pattern of the tabernacle and the pattern of all its furnishings, just so you shall make it.

GOD WILL FIND A GROUP OF REFORMERS WILLING TO CHANGE THE COURSE OF CHURCH HISTORY THROUGH SIMPLE OBEDIENCE. THEY WILL BECOME STEWARDS OF THE GREATEST MOVE OF GOD IN WORLD HISTORY—NOT SIMPLY AN AWAKENING, BUT A TRANSFORMATION OF THE PLANET.

God commanded Moses to build what was to be known as the Tabernacle of Moses. God desired to build on the earth what already existed in heaven. The Tabernacle was based on His throne room (Hebrews 8:5). Moses saw what God intended to build, and he instructed that it be built exactly as God designed it. This earthly tabernacle would be the dwelling place of God and center of life for the nation of Israel. Today, God is revealing to His children the divine order, the building plans that will reveal His glory on the earth in the same way that the Tabernacle of Moses revealed God's throne room. After nine months of work under Moses' faithful leadership, the children of Israel completed construction of the

Tabernacle exactly as God had intended. God then visited and took up residence in the place He had ordained to be built.

> And he raised up the court all around the tabernacle and the altar, and hung up the screen of the court gate. So Moses finished the work. Then the cloud covered the tabernacle of meeting, and the glory of the Lord filled the tabernacle. And Moses was not able to enter the tabernacle of meeting, because the cloud rested above it, and the glory of the Lord filled the tabernacle. Whenever the cloud was taken up from above the tabernacle, the children of Israel would go onward in all their journeys. But if the cloud was not taken up, then they did not journey till the day that it was taken up (Exodus 40:33-37).

The history of God's abiding presence in the place He ordained was not limited to the Tabernacle of Moses. It was only the beginning of a much larger story. King David set up a tent on Mount Zion to house the Ark of the Covenant, which was originally housed in the Tabernacle of Moses. Instead of sacrificing animals, the priests offered a sacrifice of praise and thanksgiving. This tent became known as the Tabernacle of David (1 Samuel 16:7, 1 Chronicles 16:27).

One day David compared the beautiful palace God had given him to the seemingly insignificant tent where His glory was dwelling, and David was filled with a desire to build a fitting temple where God's glory could dwell. God forbade it, through the prophet Nathan, saying that He intended to build a temple through David's son, Solomon (2 Samuel 7). King David spent the final years of his life helping to prepare what was needed for Solomon to build God's temple (1 Chronicles 22). When the temple was completed, God manifested His glory in a way similar to what occurred at the completion of the Tabernacle of Moses.

Indeed it came to pass, when the trumpeters and singers were as one, to make one sound to be heard in praising and thanking the Lord, and when they lifted up their voice with the trumpets and cymbals and instruments of music, and praised the Lord, saying: "For He is good, For His mercy endures forever," that the house, the house of the Lord, was filled with a cloud, so that the priests could not continue ministering because of the cloud; for the glory of the Lord filled the house of God (2 Chronicles 5:13-14).

The story of God's visitation to the temple that He ordained to be built continued in the life of His Son, Jesus Christ. God would not only come upon humanity, but delighted to *abide in* humanity for the first time in history. Jesus the Son of God, fully God and fully man, left His dwelling place in heaven. John 1:14 declares, "And the Word became flesh and dwelt among us, and we beheld His glory, the glory as of the only begotten of the Father, full of grace and truth." The glory of the Father would tabernacle in the Son, whose life on earth would reveal what God intended all of humanity to experience.

These stories of Moses, David, and Solomon building tabernacles and temples in the Old Testament illustrate what God intends for the entire human race (1 Corinthians 15:46). God's glory came to the Tabernacle of Moses because it was the place He ordained to be built. God's glory came to the Tabernacle of David because he found a man after His own heart. When the temple was completed by Solomon, God's glory came because it was His purpose for that hour in history.

As children of God, we stand at a unique threshold in history. We are the temple in which God has ordained His glory to dwell

(1 Corinthians 3:16, 1 Peter 2:5-9). Today, just as He gave Moses the blueprint for the Tabernacle, God is giving His royal priesthood on earth the blueprints for this hour so that Jesus' words may be fully realized—that God will indeed build His Church (Matthew 13:11, 16:18).

With firm conviction, I believe we will become a dwelling place for God in the earth in a way that's unique in the history of the Church and the world. Indeed, the prophetic destinies of nations hang in the balance, and God has full confidence in His people to be good stewards of the day and hour in which we live.

> WE, AS CHILDREN OF GOD, STAND AT A UNIQUE
>
> THRESHOLD IN HISTORY. WE ARE THE TEMPLE IN WHICH
>
> GOD HAS ORDAINED HIS GLORY TO DWELL.

This book is not meant to be an exhaustive study of the current shift taking place in the body of Christ. There are other voices that have arisen and will continue to rise and trumpet God's wisdom for this hour. The purpose of this book is to explore the main principles that will help us receive this shift. These principles are keys that will provide a wineskin—a wineskin of understanding that will sustain the people of God during the coming outpouring of the Holy Spirit, the likes of which the world has never seen. As we discuss God's divine design for humanity, we will explore the following themes:

- God's deep desire for intimacy as the heart and foundation of God's divine design.

- Intimacy and encounter as synergistic concepts essential to God's divine design.

- God's original intent for humanity—found in the book of Genesis and defined by the first century Church.

- Our privilege to take personal responsibility and stewardship of the earth through divine partnership with God.

- As stewards of the earth, intentionality in how we relate to God.

WE ARE WIRED FOR LOVE, AND WE WILL ONLY BE SATISFIED BY DEEP ENCOUNTERS WITH GOD. WHEN WE ENCOUNTER HIM, WE ARE TRANSFORMED INTO HIS IMAGE AND LIKENESS. WE ARE SUPPOSED TO BE THE REFLECTION OF GOD ON PLANET EARTH.

CHAPTER TWO

RESTORING THE GREATEST COMMANDMENT

It's been a particularly long day, including a full day's work, many errands, and attendance at her youngest child's soccer game—Diana is exhausted. Her one regret is missing the evening gathering at Notre Dame Stadium. Local churches had advertised a guest speaker from New York City who would share about life-transforming encounters with Jesus he'd experienced during the past year. Diana later learned that his testimony led to many experiencing their own life-transforming encounter.

Even though Diana has known the Lord since she was five years old, her recent encounters with God have been the most intimate of her life. She never imagined such a satisfying relationship with God. She takes a hot shower and heads to bed, thinking about how she misses John, who is out of town on business. It's 12:30 a.m., and she has to be up at 6:30 a.m. to begin another busy day.

Diana drifts off to sleep but is awakened moments later by a man dressed in white at the foot of her bed. Diana is startled by the man's presence but somehow not afraid. Her curiosity is piqued and she's strangely comforted as the man smiles lovingly and extends His hand in a welcoming gesture. As she takes the man's hand, the most wonderful sense of peace floods the room. She follows Him downstairs to the family room where He picks up the television remote and turns to a channel with a woman who appears to be holding a newborn baby at a hospital. Upon closer inspection she recognizes the woman as her mother, and then a man carrying flowers enters the room excitedly. It is Diana's father, and she realizes that she is observing the day of her birth. As her mother and father take turns holding her in their arms, she realizes that the man with her in the living room is also in the hospital room. Suddenly she understands that man is the Son of God, Jesus Christ! Her mother and father don't seem to notice Him, but He is the happiest person in the room—overjoyed to see the birth of this child.

Diana weeps gently as the revelation sets in that God was pleased with her even on the day of her birth. As tears run down her face, Jesus puts His arms around her. For many years she had struggled to experience her heavenly Father's love beyond an intellectual understanding. She knew God loved her because she had accepted His salvation, but she never knew that God delighted in her. In her desire to please God, she had developed spiritual disciplines and placed a priority on serving Him. But the harder she tried, the more she fell short of her "spiritual goals." Now, in this personal encounter with Jesus, years of insecurity and striving melt away. Jesus holds Diana and repeats over and over, "I have loved you with an everlasting love" (Jeremiah 31:3). Years of wrong thinking are broken by this single declaration by the Son of God.

Jesus takes a seat on the floor next to Diana, His arms still gently folded around her. He seems content to sit alongside her, enjoying her company. Before this encounter Diana never dreamed the Son of God would want to simply hang out with her. He just enjoyed her company without any need for her to perform a service for Him or strive through some spiritual activity. Diana realizes the Son of God sitting in her living room not only loves her but also wants to be her friend.

> DIANA WEEPS GENTLY AS THE REVELATION SETS IN THAT
> GOD WAS PLEASED WITH HER EVEN ON THE DAY OF HER
> BIRTH. SHE KNEW GOD LOVED HER BECAUSE SHE HAD
> ACCEPTED HIS SALVATION, BUT SHE NEVER KNEW THAT
> GOD DELIGHTED IN HER.

Diana suddenly feels the liberty to ask Jesus questions. She asks where He was during some of the most difficult times of her life. Jesus turns His face toward the television, which displays one of the most vivid scenes in Diana's life: the funeral of Jason, her younger brother. The day has always haunted her. She didn't have a chance to say good-bye when Jason died suddenly in a car accident. She weeps again as emotions of guilt and condemnation fill her soul. She notices that Jesus was present on that day also, and years of pent-up hurt and pain are once again released as Jesus puts His arms around her. His warmth and generosity amaze Diana. Enthralled by His beauty, she is filled with a desire to share His goodness with everyone. She is also amazed that her pain and sorrow melted away so easily.

Jesus and Diana remain on the living room floor watching scenes from Diana's life. Some are difficult, like the day she received a rejection letter from Princeton University, the school she dreamed of attending, but others are joyful, such as the day she married John, her college sweetheart. If she hadn't attended state university, Jesus reminds her, John would not be part of her life. Jesus appears pleased with Diana, regardless of the scene playing out in her life. Whenever a scene of pain or hurt comes up, Jesus makes it clear He is not the author of the negative circumstances. In fact, His presence brings comfort and healing as the more difficult scenes play out.

Jesus turns and looks deeply into Diana's eyes. As she gazes back, He suddenly disappears. Startled, Diana finds herself instantly back in her bed. It seems an eternity has passed since the encounter began, but the clock reveals it is only 12:30 a.m.

Diana awakes the next morning incredibly refreshed despite getting only five hours of sleep. As she moves through the day, she feels light as a feather, as if the burdens of many years have been lifted. A tangible sense of the extreme pleasure and intimacy of God remains with her. She begins to see herself the way God sees her, and she sees her students and co-workers in a different light as well. She longs for another divine encounter, for change at a deeper level. The next day she writes in her journal, "I was born to encounter God, not just once, but to experience Him during a lifetime of encounters. I will live my life to experience the pleasure of knowing God."

BORN FOR INTIMACY

From the beginning of time, God intended us to receive fulfillment through relationship—through ongoing interaction with Him. God has chosen to be friends with us and delights to unveil His goodness. We are made in the very image of God (Genesis 1:26), and His DNA resides in us. We are wired for love, and we will only be satisfied by deep encounters with God. When we encounter Him, we are transformed into His image and likeness. We are supposed to be the reflection of God on Planet Earth.

WE ARE WIRED FOR LOVE, AND WE WILL ONLY BE SATISFIED BY DEEP ENCOUNTERS WITH GOD. WHEN WE ENCOUNTER HIM, WE ARE TRANSFORMED INTO HIS IMAGE AND LIKENESS. WE ARE SUPPOSED TO BE THE REFLECTION OF GOD ON PLANET EARTH.

It's hard to hunger for something you've never tasted. One great paradigm shift that the Holy Spirit longs to reveal is the absolute joy and pleasure of experiencing God. We were designed and created for divine encounter. Our joy is found in the experience of knowing Him. Unfortunately, many who know the joy of salvation remain ignorant of the joy that comes from *walking in* their salvation. The ability to know Him is available to every person. The joy of continuous encounter with God is not an obligation or something He forces upon His followers. He simply extends an invitation of love and waits for us to respond.

The Apostle John makes this incredible assertion at the beginning of his Gospel: "But as many as received Him, to them He gave the right to become children of God, to those who believe in His name: who were born, not of blood, nor of the will of the flesh, nor of the will of man, but of God" (John 1:12-13). The word *right* in verse 12 means charge, domain, jurisdiction, and liberty. It's the same word that Gospel writers Matthew, Mark, and Luke quoted Jesus as using when He said that He had power to forgive sins (Matthew 9:6, Mark 2:10, Luke 5:24). It's also the same authority Jesus referenced in John 10:18 when He declared that He had willingly given up His life. Therefore, God has given us the power to choose if we will walk as His sons and daughters on earth.

The love of God provided this choice to humanity from the beginning of time, but a choice remains with us. A lifestyle of walking in relationship with our heavenly Father begins with a choice to meet with Him in daily encounter. God made us responsible stewards so the choices we make on earth will last forever. Therefore the choice given to us from heaven comes with divine responsibility.

Certain fundamental rights belong to us as sons and daughters of God. The first ten amendments to the U.S. Constitution were added in 1791 to protect certain rights of the citizens of the United States. In the same way, God provided His children with certain rights, empowering them to become all that He intends. Understanding these rights serves as a foundation for experiencing the pleasures of God.

THE BILL OF RIGHTS FOR SONS AND DAUGHTERS OF GOD

1. Jesus was separated from the Father so His children would not have to be. The Gospel of Luke records that Jesus sweated drops of blood in the garden of Gethsemane (Luke 22:40). Thinking of the physical pain He would experience through crucifixion was reason enough for Jesus to sweat blood, but it was not the only reason. He also knew the sin and guilt of the world would soon be placed upon Him. Jesus would bear the judgment of God that humanity deserved. The judgment required the Son to be separated from the Father. Mark 15:34 declares, "… at the ninth hour Jesus cried out with a loud voice, saying, 'Eloi Eloi, lama sabachthani?' which is translated, "My God, My God, why have You forsaken Me?"

OUR REASON FOR LIVING IS TO EXPERIENCE THE
GLORY OF COMMUNION WITH THE FATHER.

God the Father allowed the Son to experience the judgment and suffering of the world so we would not have to die in our sins. Not only this, but He has restored to us the ability to walk in the glory that God intended before the foundation of the world (Hebrews 2:9-10). Our reason for living is to experience the glory of communion with the Father. A wonderful exchange took place at the cross. Jesus received the judgment humanity deserved so we could experience the glory Jesus has experienced since the foundation of the earth. The cross was sufficient. Sons and daughters of God would never need to be separated from the Father. Our religious works could never make us right with God. Similarly, our religious works can't bring us any closer to Him. Everything that will ever be done to make us right with God has taken place on the cross. God even views our weaknesses and errors through the finished work of Jesus on the cross.

After Adam and Eve chose to sin, they hid themselves from God (Genesis 3:8). In the parable of the prodigal son, the young man returns to his father after spending all the inheritance his father had given him. He returns, but only with the expectation of serving as a slave in his father's house (Luke 15:11-32). Today many sons and daughters can identify with these experiences. They missed the mark and feel unworthy to enter the Father's presence.

The opposite is true as we understand what Jesus accomplished on the cross. The Son was separated from the Father so we would never have to experience separation. The Father's presence is the only place that can redeem us and the only rightful place for us to return. While the prodigal may have traveled far from his father's house, he was not far from his inheritance sealed with the father. Thus the writer of Hebrews admonishes, "Let us therefore come boldly to the throne of grace, that we may obtain mercy and find grace to help in time of need" (Hebrews 4:16).

God designed us with a deep need for relationship with Him, so He also provided a way to have continuous access to the place where that need is met: His presence. Our message to the world should be birthed from the revelation that in your current situation and choices, you are not far from the Father's presence. As sons and daughters we live with the answer to all of life's problems. The seed of heaven resides within us, offering hope to everyone around us. As the Apostle Paul wrote,

> God was in Christ reconciling the world to Himself, not imputing their trespasses to them, and has committed to us the word of reconciliation (2 Corinthians 5:19).

2. Jesus' death on the cross made us new creatures. The Apostle Paul declared in 2 Corinthians 5:17, "Therefore, if anyone is in Christ, he is a new creation, old things have passed away; all things have become new." This statement is vital to understanding our inheritance as sons and daughters. A new era has dawned in how God relates to humanity. That word "new" in Greek does not merely mean recent (which is expressed by a different Greek word, see Revelation 21:1).[1] "New" implies a nature quite different from anything previously existing. This new era pertains to the entire human race. The good news of the Kingdom of God means heaven has erased your past, and now you are a citizen of heaven. Complete

---

[1]Jamieson, Robert; Fausset, A. R.; Fausset, A. R.; Brown, David; Brown, David: *A Commentary, Critical and Explanatory, on the Old and New Testaments.* Oak Harbor, WA : Logos Research Systems, Inc., 1997, S. 2 Co 5:17

surrender is what opens the door into the Kingdom of God and now as a citizen of heaven, the Father desires to make all things new (Philippians 3:20).

In Genesis 2:7 God breathed into humanity the breath of life. God breathed humanity into existence. Adam's sin separated us from experiencing the fullness of God's breath in our lives. But God would not be denied having His creation experience His fullness. After Jesus' death and resurrection, He appeared to His disciples and breathed the Holy Spirit on them (John 20:22). This life-giving breath of God signified a shift in the way God would relate to man. His breath is the glorious inheritance of every child of God. Not only has God restored us to His original design, but He has now given us a more glorious place. In the garden, God walked with man. Today, God dwells *within* man. We have become His dwelling place.

The Apostle Paul wrote:

And so it is written, "The first man Adam became a living being. The last Adam became a life-giving spirit" (1 Corinthians 15:45).

Many of God's children continue to struggle with harmful mindsets, practices, and lifestyle choices, prompting them to question whether God has really made them new creatures. On the day one is born again, no child of God is fully developed. While God places us in community (the church), each child of God also has their own individual journey with the Father. At different junctures in time, we each enter into experiences with truth that help us live out our new nature. Some believers live out aspects of their new nature sooner than others. Each son and daughter of God is a work in progress.

John and Ricky: Works in Progress

John and Ricky have been best friends for ten years. Invited by a mutual acquaintance, they both end up at Encounter Community Church one Sunday morning. As the service comes to a close, the pastor explains the plan of salvation and offers to pray for anyone who would like to respond. John and Ricky both pray and surrender their lives to Jesus. As John prays to receive Jesus into his heart, he begins to speak in tongues, evidence that he has been baptized in the Holy Spirit (Acts 2:4). Ricky does not speak in tongues when he is praying, but he does have a significant encounter with the Father. As he's praying, he feels a warmth that begins in his head and goes down his back and into his legs. After three years of enduring pain in his legs, Ricky's body is healed in a moment.

John and Ricky both became new creatures on this glorious day. However, at the moment of salvation, they experienced different facets of the Kingdom of God. Ricky experienced Christ as healer, and John experienced Jesus as baptizer in the Holy Spirit. The fact that Ricky did not experience the same thing as John and vice versa does not mean the same experience wasn't available. God simply desired to give them experiences of Himself that were missing from their knowledge of God.

The same is true of children of God who still struggle with sinful habits. Their experience of sin does not negate the new nature the Father has bestowed upon them. The door to the Father's house is always open to give you an experience of truth that will allow you to live out the reality of your new nature. The Father longs to walk with us and mature us so that we can fully experience the inheritance He has reserved for us. Jesus said it well:

If you abide in My word, you are My disciples indeed. And you shall know the truth, and the truth shall make you free (John 8:31-32).

3. Jesus desires for us to relate to the Father as He related to the Father. There is a synergy that exists in how the Godhead relates to each other. We find a pattern throughout Scripture of how the three Persons of God function and operate together. It was the Word of God, Jesus, that formed the universe (Genesis 1). It was the Father that declared His love over the Son at His baptism (Matthew 3:17). God does not give the Spirit with measure; the Spirit never left Jesus to fulfill that which God destined him to accomplish. And it was the Holy Spirit who filled the disciples on the day of Pentecost. Although we see distinct operations of the three Persons of the Trinity, it is still one God. The doctrine of the Trinity is indeed a mystery that cannot be fathomed by human intellect.

Jesus prayed that we would come to know this wondrous mystery. In John 17 Jesus prayed what many have described as His high priestly prayer. "I desire that they all may be one, as You, Father, are in Me, and I in You; that they also may be one in Us, that the world may believe that You sent Me" (John 17:21).

Jesus left the Father and humbled Himself, taking the form of man, so that humanity could be redeemed. But Jesus did not forsake the oneness that existed between Himself and the Father. Jesus was most certainly fully God and fully man when He walked the earth. He related to the Father as a man in right relationship with God. Jesus became the model for every son and daughter, and His union with the Father is now our inheritance.

The reason Jesus prayed for His followers to be one as He and His Father were one was quite simple: "That the world may believe."

An understanding of our union with the Father is essential for the world to believe.

> And the glory which You gave Me I have given them, that they may be one just as We are one (John 17:22).

The word used for glory can also be translated splendor, brightness, shining, radiance,[2] and honor. Therefore, the same honor and glory the Father bestowed upon Jesus has now been given to each of us. Jesus' life and ministry were a result of the glory the Father allowed Him to see when He walked the earth (John 5:19), culminating in a shift that changed the earth forever.

> JESUS PRAYED FOR HIS FOLLOWERS TO BE ONE AS HE AND HIS FATHER WERE ONE, SO "THAT THE WORLD MAY BELIEVE." AN UNDERSTANDING OF OUR UNION WITH THE FATHER IS ESSENTIAL FOR THE WORLD TO BELIEVE.

All of heaven longs for the sons and daughters of God to perceive what the Father has given them. Many of God's children strive for what has already been freely given by grace! The question must be asked: If I've been given the same glory that Jesus had when He walked the earth, how could I need anything else? Jesus declared that the Father freely shows Him all things. So also the Father longs to share all things with us (John 5:20).

Another facet of the glory that was bestowed on Jesus is seen in how He related to God specifically as Father. God longs to relate to us as His dear children. Jesus declared that in order to enter the

---

[2] Swanson, James: *Dictionary of Biblical Languages With Semantic Domains: Greek (New Testament)*. Electronic ed. Oak Harbor: Logos Research Systems, Inc., 1997, S. DBLG 1518, #2

Kingdom of God, we must become like little children (Matthew 18:2-3). Jesus modeled this behavior in His life, continually addressing God as Father. When His disciples asked for instruction on how to pray, Jesus said they should begin their communion with God by addressing Him as Father (Matthew 6:9).

When children relate properly to their parents, they have absolute confidence that their parents love them and will always provide for them. This confidence is instinctive as they feel the love of their parents. Our confidence as children of God is rooted in the same love He had for His eternal Son. Jesus concludes His high priestly prayer, "… I have declared to them Your name, and will declare it, that the love with which You loved Me may be in them, and I in them" (John 17:26). As children of God we are never to allow our weakness or negativity to destroy our confidence in the Father. God is unchanging in His love and favor toward us, even when we are learning to work out our salvation.

GOD WILL REBUILD THE FOUNDATION

To transition into what God intends for us in this hour, we must make relationship with Him our highest priority. Heaven is releasing a clear word that will shift the body of Christ and the nations. When sons and daughters engage in vital relationship with their Father, the foundation is laid for them to hear what God desires for His people right now.

Any builder will understand the importance of a strong foundation for the long-term stability of a structure. When even a small portion of the foundation becomes compromised, the integrity of the whole structure is weakened. You can patch the foundation, but unless the cracked portion is removed the structure will still be weakened. Just as the foundation sustains the weight of the entire structure, the Father is building a strong foundation from which we can receive the inheritance that was purchased by the blood of Jesus. It is an inheritance of fruitfulness beyond anything the body of Christ has yet experienced. The Father, in His mercy, will not release it until the appropriate foundation has been laid.

Jesus will return for a pure and spotless Bride—His representatives of heaven and reflectors of His glory. Our intimacy with Him is the foundation that will release His glory. We, the people of God, can no longer ignore cracks in the Church's foundation. Deficits have emerged because of a lack of knowledge of God's ways. These foundational deficits limit the glory God desires to release through us and compromise our ability to be what Jesus intends us to be, namely, a city set on hill and a light that can not be hid (Matthew 5:14).

We know that God, in His great love for humanity, will ultimately repair the Church's foundational deficits. As the Apostle Paul declares, Jesus Christ is the chief cornerstone of the Church (Ephesians 2:20). Indeed, belief in the Son of God will become the chief cornerstone in the Church's foundation. God is going to raise up a remnant of believers in this final hour who are committed to the greatest commandment, loving God with all their heart, mind, soul and strength.

In Matthew 22 a Pharisee lawyer asks Jesus, " 'Teacher, which is the great commandment in the law?' Jesus said to him, 'You shall love the Lord your God with all your heart, with all your soul, and with all your mind'" (Matthew 22:36-37). This wasn't a new question. The scribes had been debating it for centuries. They had documented 613 commandments in the Law, 248 positive and 365 negative.

No one could ever hope to obey all of these commandments.

JESUS WILL RETURN FOR A PURE AND SPOTLESS
BRIDE—HIS REPRESENTATIVES OF HEAVEN AND
REFLECTORS OF HIS GLORY. OUR INTIMACY WITH HIM
IS THE FOUNDATION THAT WILL RELEASE HIS GLORY.

So, to make it easier, the experts divided the commandments into "heavy" (important) and "light" (unimportant). A person could major in the "heavy commandments" and not worry about the trivial ones.[3] While we in the body of Christ may not have "heavy" or "light" commandments, we certainly engage in a lot of activity designed to please God and reach the world with the gospel. We may want to ask ourselves what we should major in. How should we love Him with all our heart, soul, and strength?

Jesus responded to the rich young ruler by quoting the Shema (Deuteronomy 6:4), a statement of faith that was recited daily by every orthodox Jew. (The word *Shema* comes from the Hebrew word meaning "to hear.")[4] But love for God cannot be divorced from love for one's neighbor, so Jesus also quoted Leviticus 19:18 and put it on the same level as the Shema. All of the Law and the Prophets hang on *both* of these commandments.[5] Our love for God is demonstrated by our love for our neighbor. In other words, the truth of our beliefs must be demonstrated tangibly. This was the scriptural standard clearly articulated by Jesus. What the orthodox Jew recited

---

[3]Wiersbe, W. W. 1996, c1989. *The Bible Exposition Commentary,* An exposition of the New Testament comprising the entire "BE" series. Victor Books: Wheaton, Ill.

[4]Wiersbe, Warren W.: *The Bible Exposition Commentary.* Wheaton, Ill.: Victor Books, 1996, c1989, S. Mt 22:34

[5] Wiersbe, Warren W.: *The Bible Exposition Commentary.* Wheaton, Ill.: Victor Books, 1996, c1989, S. Mt 22:34

on a daily basis was what they were to become. The same principle applies to us. In Matthew 22:20 Jesus says that we are to become a living, breathing statement of faith.

THE EXPERIENCE THAT TRANSFORMS

We are a people with a message, but the deep desire of heaven is to make us a people with a lifestyle that matches our message. Martin Luther's liberating message of grace through faith was birthed out of his personal experience with the saving truth of the gospel. The twelve Apostles were commanded to preach that the Kingdom of Heaven was at hand, but only after they personally encountered the King of that Kingdom (Luke 6:13, 9:1-2).

> WE ARE A PEOPLE WITH A MESSAGE, BUT THE
> DEEP DESIRE OF HEAVEN IS TO MAKE US A PEOPLE
> WITH A LIFESTYLE THAT MATCHES OUR MESSAGE.

Enoch walked with God all the days of his life. He *became* God's message and so pleased God that he was translated into heaven (Genesis 5:24). The Apostle Peter became the message, and his shadow healed the sick (Acts 5:15), but only after many hard life lessons. God's purpose for divine encounter is for us to become the image of bearers of Christ, demonstrating the hope of His glory (Colossians 1:27). Jesus, as our example, certainly proclaimed the message of the "good news" but the course of history was changed because He was the message. The portals of heaven are open for the people of God to become the message—a statement of faith to the world around us.

God describes those who believe in Him as the body of Christ, His dear children (Galatians 4:6-7, Romans 8:15), and the Bride of Christ (Ephesians 5:22-23). These three metaphors demonstrate God's desire to mature us through personal encounter.

The covenant of marriage is consummated when a man and woman declare their intention to commit wholeheartedly to each other. In the same way, surrendering to God releases all the resources God has given freely to His children. What's more, these Kingdom resources can only be received through the door of divine encounter—and not a one-time event, but a lifestyle of encounter that will continue in eternity (John 17:3). When a marriage is consummated, the man and woman know each other in a more unique and intimate way than ever before. For the covenant to remain strong, they must continually renew their commitment and pursue each other in intimacy. Similarly, God invites His children to know Him in a unique way through a lifestyle of encounter. A marriage void of ongoing intimacy is unhealthy and of questionable duration. The same applies to our relationship with God.

We were all infants at one time, and we become like infants again when we're born into the family of God. Even in this "infantile" state, we already have all the resources needed to become fully grown believers. A lifestyle of consistent encounter with heaven will mature us into the people God intends for us to be. The Apostle Paul articulates God's desire for our maturity when he writes,

I keep asking that the God of our Lord Jesus Christ, the glorious Father, may give you the Spirit of wisdom and revelation, so that you may know him better. I pray that the eyes of your heart may be enlightened in order that you may know the hope to which he has called you, the riches of his glorious inheritance in his holy people, and his incomparably great power for us who believe. That power is the same as the mighty strength (Ephesians 1:17-19, NIV).

History's greatest invitation has been given to humanity, namely, to know Him. As we see life through the prism of heaven's perspective, we will co-labor with Christ and influence history. Let me offer some principles for stewarding the greatest invitation ever given.

PRINCIPLES FOR LOVING GOD

1. Take Personal Responsibility. Choosing to love God is perhaps the greatest privilege we have as sons and daughters of God. God's commitment to our free will is embodied by His choice to make us stewards of the earth (Psalm 115:16). But with our great privilege comes the great accountability we will have on the day of judgment (2 Corinthians 5:9-11). So we must take personal responsibility for developing our history with God. Your personal history with God will determine your future. The Apostle Paul said it best when he declared, "Therefore, my dear friends, as you have always obeyed—not only in my presence, but now much more in my absence—continue to work out your salvation with fear and trembling" (Philippians 2:12).

2. Draw Near to Him. Heaven applauds as we draw near to God. He has done everything possible to enable us to know Him. What we hunger for we will pursue, and God has promised to reveal Himself to the hungry (Matthew 5:6).

If you come near to God, He will come near to you. Wash your hands, you sinners, and purify your hearts, you double-minded (James 4:7-8, NIV).

As the Bride of Christ, we were fashioned to come alive as we draw near to Him. Drawing near to God is not a one-time act, but something from which all our life springs. The writer of Hebrews declares that faith is a necessary ingredient to pleasing God and that He rewards those who diligently seek Him (Hebrews 11:6).

PRACTICAL GUIDELINES FOR DRAWING NEAR TO GOD

- **Worship.** Play your favorite worship songs and worship along. Psalm 22 says that God inhabits the praises of His people. Recognize that worship is a lifestyle. Our lives become a pleasing fragrance to God through each act of submission, repentance, and obedience.

- **Meditate On and Confess Scripture.** Meditate on the Scripture and speak back to God what He was declared about you (Joshua 1). One key to walking out the truths of the Kingdom involves abiding in God's word. Jesus told the Jews who believed in Him that they would know the truth, and the truth would set them free (John 8:31-32).

- **Take Time to Listen.** Take concentrated, focused time to ask the Father what He is speaking to you. God delights in talking with His children. Jesus declared that man lives by the words that proceed from the mouth of God (Matthew 4:4). We will look closer at developing our ability to "hear" God at the end of this chapter.

- **Engage in Bible Study.** It's unfortunate to find believers who devote hours to planning and researching life decisions but never think to develop a Bible study plan. Bible study is a spiritual discipline required to draw near to God. As you read, ask the Holy Spirit to open the words of life and show you things you've never seen. Quantity doesn't equal quality when it comes to time spent in scriptural study. God may invite you to meditate on a particular verse over and over for weeks or even months. God will emphasize different themes in Scripture according to the seasons of life we're navigating. Ask God to help you develop a biblical worldview and show you how He is present in your sphere of influence. I've discovered—like many things in the Christian life—the more you study Scripture the more you are filled with awe at God (Proverbs 29:18).

- **Interact.** As we draw near to God, we discover the privilege of being His friend. God has called us as co-laborers with Him to release His will on the earth. As I've labored alongside God, I've learned to ask Him to share His thoughts, strategies, and prayer instructions with me. Those who interact with our Father in heaven will bear the most fruit in the next move of God, receiving reliable guidance that flows out of relationship, not a rulebook of commands.

> THOSE WHO INTERACT WITH OUR FATHER IN HEAVEN WILL BEAR THE MOST FRUIT IN THE NEXT MOVE OF GOD, RECEIVING RELIABLE GUIDANCE THAT FLOWS OUT OF RELATIONSHIP, NOT A RULEBOOK OF COMMANDS.

- **Record.** We should record what we believe God speaks to us each day. As I've recorded what the Lord says to me, He has honored my small steps of faithfulness by *continuing* to speak with me. As I write down what I believe God says through the day and in my dreams at night, God seems to talk even more clearly to me on a daily basis. Use whatever is convenient to record—I take my iPad with me everywhere. As you diligently record what you believe God is saying and you learn His voice, you can begin to share it with those around you. Our friends, spiritual leaders, and others contribute to our ability to hear the voice of God and help enable that voice to navigate how we live our lives.

- **Learn the Rest of Faith.** Many sons and daughters of God carry heavy burdens and endure harsh circumstances. This was never God's intention for us. Jesus never promised a problem-free life. In fact, He promised that we would encounter trouble in the world! But we can be happy in the midst of trouble because He has overcome the world (John 16:33). The "rest" we can enjoy in Christ begins by releasing our need for control and allowing God to direct our lives. When we declare our confidence in God, we release Him to become Lord of every situation. But our rest will only come about as we experience authentic encounters with God. Jesus implores us to take His yoke and learn from Him (Matthew 11:29). Far too many of God's children seem burdened down with life's challenges. Although they profess faith in God, they don't trust with absolute confidence His ability to see them through.

Therefore, since a promise remains of entering His rest, let us fear lest any of you seem to have come short of it (Hebrews 4:1).

TWO MORE PRINCIPLES FOR HEARING GOD'S VOICE

1. God Speaks in the Context of Communion. The first book of the Bible describes how the first two human beings heard the sound of the Lord's voice in the cool of day (Genesis 3:8). This story from the garden unveils one of the greatest privileges we have as sons and daughters: our ability to hear the voice of God. All of humanity possesses the potential to hear God's voice because we are made in His image. Even before we submit to God, we already have the ability to hear the voice of the Lord. We responded to that voice when we were born again (Romans 10:17). Now, as His dear children, He will certainly speak as we draw near to Him. Consistent communion allows us to discern God's voice so we can receive the daily direction and spiritual sustenance we so desperately need. God desires that all His children hear His voice so they can be empowered and equipped to understand the mysteries of the Kingdom (Matthew 13:11). This takes place when we become good stewards of what we hear:

> For whoever has, to him more will be given, and he will have abundance; but whoever does not have, even what he has will be taken away from him (Matthew 13:12).

2. Learn to Distinguish the Sound and Rhythm of God's Voice. Jesus promised that His sheep would hear His voice (John 10:27). But while each of us can hear God's voice, the way He relates to each of us will be different and unique. For example, you wouldn't speak to a toddler the same way you'd speak to a teenager. Similarly, though my sister and I both have wonderful relationships with my father and he says certain things to us in a similar manner, the way he *relates* to us is different and unique. This speaks to the wonder and privilege of serving the one true God. There are nearly

> GOD WILL SPEAK TO YOU WITH A PARTICULAR
> SOUND AND RHYTHM, SOMETHING RECOGNIZABLE
> ONLY BETWEEN THE TWO OF YOU. LEARNING TO
> DISCERN THE VOICE OF GOD IS VITALLY IMPORTANT
> IF WE ARE TO FULFILL HIS DESTINY FOR OUR LIVES.

five billion people living on earth, and God desires to have a unique and personal relationship with each of them.

While the basic principles of distinguishing the voice of God can be taught, no one can tell you exactly how He will speak to you. The practice of hearing God's voice can only be learned through personal experience. He will speak to you with a particular sound and rhythm, something recognizable only between the two of you. Learning to discern the voice of God is vitally important if we are to fulfill His destiny for our lives.

GOD IS RESTORING THE TABERNACLE OF DAVID IN OUR DAY. NO MORE WILL GOD'S CHILDREN GATHER ONCE A WEEK FOR A FEW HOURS; RATHER IT WILL TURN INTO MEETINGS THAT NEVER END AS THE CHILDREN OF GOD ENCOUNTER THE BEAUTY OF LORD! OUR SERVICES WILL BREAK OUT INTO CONTINUOUS WORSHIP AND PRAYER CELEBRATIONS.

CHAPTER THREE

REBUILDING THE TABERNACLE OF DAVID

It's Day 90 of the spiritual phenomenon that's taking place at Notre Dame Stadium—spontaneous gatherings of believers show up nightly to worship and praise God. One night recently, the gathering seemed to be drawing to a close when suddenly, thousands erupted into a spontaneous prophetic song that shook the stadium like a vast heavenly choir. More and more people poured into the stadium as the song of the Lord continued. University of Notre Dame school officials were forced to allow the gatherings to continue because no other venue was big enough to contain the crowd. The mayor and city common council also encouraged the university officials to allow the meetings to continue because of the positive effects taking place throughout the community. The very atmosphere seems to have changed, they said. The city of South Bend provides local police and other personnel to manage the event, and a group of local businessmen have banded together to support the events financially, some of whom don't even claim any religious affiliation but were nevertheless moved to help out with the cost of what's being referred to as "God's meeting."

The stadium worship celebrations have been going on continuously twenty-four hours a day and seven days a week. Many thousands in attendance come under the influence of the Holy Spirit and never even make it to their seats. A special section was set up on the right side of stage for those who are unable to walk or simply want to rest in the Holy Spirit's presence. Sometimes a local pastor or guest minister preaches, but the worship always continues quietly in the background. Worship teams and bands from across the region lead people in spontaneous worship and intercession. Since the meetings are continuous, local church leaders have coordinated seamlessly as one new man to support what God's doing, and the worship teams may consist of a complete band or one individual, both of whom lead thousands into worship each night.

The character of the worship varies with the personality and genre of those leading it, releasing a unique heavenly sound every night. Prophets had spoken of a move of God where the unique sounds of heavenly worship would be released and hearts would turn back to God. Now the prophetic words are beginning to be fulfilled through this outpouring of the Holy Spirit where it seems that sounds never heard before are released into the stadium each night as the people of God enter into worship.

The heavenly sounds have created an environment where encounters with God are commonplace. And it doesn't seem to be limited by geography. Reports from miles away describe people going into trances—life-changing experiences like the Apostle Paul's conversion in Acts 10. Others report hearing audible voices telling them to go to the stadium and meet with God.

GOD DESIRES A PLACE ON EARTH THAT'S A LOT LIKE HEAVEN,
WHERE WORSHIP AND PRAYER ARE RELEASED CONTINUOUSLY.

A diversity of media outlets has captured these happenings. Local Church leaders set up cameras throughout the stadium on the tenth day to capture what God was doing each evening. The meetings are webcast around the world from 7 p.m. until 1 a.m., with as many as 500,000 logging on to participate.

A great majority—though not all—of local Christian leaders have embraced what God is doing. This majority represents every major denomination and stream in the body of Christ. However, some leaders have been asked to leave their group or denomination because of their support of the movement.

Those embracing the outpouring have found many of the paradigms and structures in their local assemblies to be incongruous with what God is doing. Leaders have experienced great blessings in their local congregations as they've embraced and supported the stadium gatherings. The harvest of souls coming into the Kingdom in the city of South Bend is beyond anyone's imagination. Even the city's largest churches can't contain the crowds that visit on Sunday morning. A local newspaper described church as the most popular place to be. The rapid church growth has caused leaders to band together, providing spiritual leadership for the city, not just their local assemblies.

Church leaders agreed to never make a decision concerning the outpouring without spending three days in prayer together. As they sought God's guidance, it became clear that this was not a seasonal or regional outpouring but part of a global outpouring that God is using to transform nations. Not every question has been answered when it comes to managing this outpouring of the Holy Spirit, but one thing has been made perfectly clear: God desires a place on earth that's a lot like heaven, where worship and prayer are released continuously.

A number of church buildings in the area now remain open around the clock to accommodate the devotional needs of the community. At the heart of this continuous worship and intercession is a Bride—the Bride of Christ—falling passionately in love with the Lord Jesus in ever-increasing measure.

OUR CHARGE: FOLLOW HEAVEN'S ROADMAP

Is it possible that our beautiful churches and stunning cathedrals—with thousands of seats —were meant to be filled more often than once or twice a week? Perhaps God has a greater purpose. A time is coming when the largest churches will be unable to contain the harvest of new believers coming into the Kingdom. Is it possible that the worldwide church was intended to exercise much greater influence and authority in the world than it does today? Were outpourings of the past meant for a season or did God intend something with lasting fruit? Can it be that an hour approaches when the glory of God will cover the earth as waters cover the sea? Is there a more effective strategy to take us into God's purposes for the Church in this hour?

A number of God's priorities for earth have yet to be fulfilled. God promised to pour out His Spirit on all flesh (Joel 2:28). God promised the whole earth would be filled with the knowledge of His glory (Habakkuk 2:14). Jesus promised we would do greater works than He Himself (John 14:12). I believe God not only released these promises to us but also provided a roadmap to fulfill them so we can enter into our heaven-ordained inheritance.

God is establishing a Church that is without blemish, victorious, and fully engaged in destroying the works of the enemy (Ephesians 5:27, Matthew 16:18). He has equipped us for victory, but we must follow heaven's roadmap to change the course of history. We must avoid the greatest potential pitfall of our day: being endowed with an anointing but falling short because we haven't followed the strategy provided by heaven. The strategies which brought us victory in the past may not suffice for this present season. We must be open to change. God is doing a new thing.

> A NUMBER OF GOD'S PRIORITIES FOR EARTH HAVE YET TO BE FULFILLED. GOD PROMISED TO POUR OUT HIS SPIRIT ON ALL FLESH. GOD PROMISED THE WHOLE EARTH WOULD BE FILLED WITH THE KNOWLEDGE OF HIS GLORY. GOD PROMISED WE WOULD DO GREATER WORKS THAN HE HIMSELF.

Just as Jesus turned water into wine during the wedding at Cana, serving the best wine last, God is once again reserving the best wine—the greatest Holy Spirit outpouring the world has ever known—for this final hour of history. God is preparing new wineskins to contain this glorious new wine.

The new wineskins may seem strange. God is preparing new modes of operation and a new ordering of priorities that will expose the atrophied structure of the Church. Only that which is built on the original strong foundation of the Church will endure. Only that which is birthed by God will continue to stand. He has called us into a glorious Kingdom that confronts the darkness of this world (Colossians 1:13). This requires us to be firmly rooted, standing on the foundation of an unshakable Kingdom (Hebrews 12:26-27). We can't expect to destroy darkness in our own strength—the weapons of our warfare are not carnal (2 Corinthians 10:4-5). Heaven desires to redefine what it means to live in the victory and fruitfulness the Father intends for us.

A paradigm is a set of assumptions, concepts, values, and practices that define the way we view reality. Paradigms help shape the culture, mindsets, and beliefs of a particular group. The paradigm shift God is bringing will produce a Church capable of shaping the nations of the earth.

God is challenging the consumer-driven culture of Western Christianity where most churches have been created to satisfy the needs of people. It is not uncommon to find churches taking surveys of their communities, asking what they are looking for in a local church body.

But when the consumer's need becomes the goal, the majority of our time and energy is spent trying to meet that need. The parishioner then becomes the client who must be "sold" on the product, the local church. If the client feels comfortable with the product, they will return. Weekend services are the product presentation and the pinnacle of church marketing, with each service carefully timed and prescribed to the comfort of those in attendance. The gospel must be presented in a way that's "culturally relevant," and those who are "born again" must be provided with the same comfortable cultural environment in order to nurture and grow their faith.

The spirit of fear perpetuates the consumer church culture. Leaders fear a lack of numeric growth if they don't create a user-friendly environment—one that meets the needs of the people. That's the lie of consumer-driven church culture—that numerical growth is the primary indicator of success. Those with the best numbers are deemed most successful, and therefore those who exercise the greatest influence over universal church leadership. This influence perpetuates the consumer-driven culture, often resulting in larger gatherings of people. The problem with this is two-fold: leaders without understanding overemphasize a one-dimensional measure of success, and the spirit of fear hijacks the Church to endorse a consumer culture rather than equipping saints for the work of ministry.

Meeting the needs of people and church growth are elements of Kingdom culture, but they were never meant to dominate our thought processes as a people. Jesus implores Peter to feed His sheep (John 21:17), and Luke chronicles the explosive growth of the New Testament Church in the Book of Acts.

The early Church experienced unprecedented growth and exerted great influence on the society in which they lived. Scholars estimate that the early Church experienced 200% growth rates—120 believers grew to 100,000 believers in just thirty years (Wagner Commentary). This growth rate has never been repeated in Church history.

In addition to growth, the early Church experienced something else rarely witnessed in the annals of history: a demonstration of fruitful results from preaching the gospel similar to what Jesus experienced when He preached. The lame walked, the sick were healed, the dead were raised, and cities were shaken by the authority and dominion of God (Acts 13:44).

IN ADDITION TO EXPONENTIAL GROWTH, THE EARLY CHURCH EXPERIENCED SOMETHING ELSE RARELY WITNESSED IN THE ANNALS OF HISTORY: THE LAME WALKED, THE SICK WERE HEALED, THE DEAD WERE RAISED, AND CITIES WERE SHAKEN BY THE AUTHORITY AND DOMINION OF GOD.

The growth and apostolic witness of the early Church is a picture of what God wants to accomplish in this hour. The desire of heaven is rooted in the final words of Jesus, spoken to His disciples in the book of Matthew:

And Jesus came and spoke to them, saying, "All authority has been given to Me in heaven and on earth. Go therefore and make disciples of all the nations, baptizing them in the name of the Father and of the Son and of the Holy Spirit, teaching them to observe all things that I have commanded you; and lo, I am with you always, *even* to the end of the age. Amen" (Matthew 28:16-20).

Jesus' command to disciple nations must have seemed daunting to the eleven stunned disciples assembled on this mountain in Galilee. In fact the text indicates some doubted even as they worshipped Him. But Jesus provided a roadmap for the disciples to be clothed with His power and authority and anointed to disciple nations. The roadmap included the assurance that He would always be with them. He also told them not to leave Jerusalem until they received the promised baptism of the Holy Spirit (Acts 1:4-5). By following this command, they were filled with the Spirit and followed in the footsteps of Jesus, who only did what He saw His Father in heaven doing.

The Book of Acts documents the early Church's continual devotion to prayer. Prayer can be likened to humanity's need for food and water for survival, and we must become a people like the early Church who recognize the vital need to partner with God in prayer. Prayer opens the door to life-changing encounters! The Apostles understood this firsthand, having observed the power that came from Jesus' continuous connection with His Father. Jesus declared that He would build His Church (Matthew 16:18) through divine partnership. The Apostles extended the Kingdom of God through divine partnership with heaven. They were constantly given to prayer. When persecution arose, the Apostles prayed for courage to be a witness for Christ, and the entire room was shaken (Acts 4:23-31) and eventually, the world. The normalcy of prayer and divine encounter appears throughout the narrative of the early Church:

- Stephen prayed as he was being stoned (Acts 2:42-47; 3:1; 6:4).

- Peter and John prayed for the Samaritans (Acts 8:14–17).

- Saul of Tarsus prayed after his conversion (Acts 9:11).

- Peter prayed before he raised Dorcas from the dead (Acts 9:36–43).

- Cornelius prayed that God would show him how to be saved (Acts 10:1–4), and Peter was on the housetop praying when God showed him how to be the answer to Cornelius' prayers (Acts 10:9).

- The believers in John Mark's house prayed for Peter when he was in prison, and the Lord delivered him from both prison and death (Acts 12:1–11).

- The church at Antioch fasted and prayed before sending out Barnabas and Paul (Acts 13:1–3, and note 14:23).

- At a prayer meeting in Philippi, God opened Lydia's heart (Acts 16:13), and at another prayer meeting in Philippi prison doors were opened (Acts 16:25).

- Paul prayed for his friends before leaving them (Acts 20:36; 21:5).

- In the midst of a storm, Paul prayed for God's blessing (Acts 27:35), and after a storm he prayed that God would heal a sick man (Acts 28:8).

A lifestyle of prayer is what allowed the early Church to thrive in the midst of great persecution. Demonstration of the gospel included outstanding miracles and an increase in the number of those being added to the Church (Acts 5). In recognizing their great need for God, the early Church became the most influential institution in human history. What began with 120 people in a prayer room quickly spread into a worldwide movement that was perfectly in sync with the rhythms of heaven, not necessarily the culture of the day.

WHAT BEGAN WITH 120 PEOPLE IN A PRAYER ROOM QUICKLY SPREAD INTO A WORLDWIDE MOVEMENT THAT WAS PERFECTLY IN SYNC WITH THE RHYTHMS OF HEAVEN, NOT NECESSARILY THE CULTURE OF THE DAY.

The roadmap for this unprecedented time on earth included making encounter with God their first priority, enabling the early Church to become a people who could disciple nations. The same roadmap is available to us in this hour. God wants to partner with His children to win victories previously thought impossible.

I was attending The Call, a solemn assembly, in Washington, D.C. on August 16, 2008, when I heard the Lord speak to me clearly, "Without twenty-four hour worship and prayer there will be no Church reformation." I believe the location where this was spoken, our capitol, was significant. God wants to release His governmental power into the nations through worship and intercession. Once again, the early Church is our pattern, offering a glimpse of a paradigm marked by twenty-four hour worship and prayer.

One of the great turning points for the early Church occurs in Acts 15. In a meeting known as the Jerusalem Council, the Apostles and elders met to consider the question of adherence to the Law of Moses by Gentile believers in Jesus.

And with this the words of the prophets agree, just as it is written: "After this I will return and will rebuild the Tabernacle of David, which has fallen down; I will rebuild its ruins, and I will set it up; so that the rest of mankind may seek the Lord, even all the Gentiles who are called by My name," says the Lord who does all these things. Known to God from eternity are all His works (Acts 15:15-18).

After a discussion, which included Apostles Peter, Paul, and James the brother of Jesus, the group decided that no further requirement (e.g., the Law of Moses) should be made of the Gentiles. James quoted Amos' prophecy (Amos 9:11-12) that God would rebuild David's fallen tent. The prophecy of Amos was being fulfilled through the coming together of Jew and Gentile as one new man in the worship of Jesus Christ.

To understand the implications of this fulfillment of prophecy, we need to understand the context of David's fallen tent. Around 100 B.C., King David commanded that the Levites carry the Ark of the Covenant into the capitol of Jerusalem in the midst of celebration with songs and musical instruments and dancing. David then placed the Ark of the Covenant in a tent and appointed eighty-eight prophetic singers and 4,000 musicians to minister to the Lord. As David performed his duties as king, he appointed Levites to worship twenty-four hours a day, seven days a week. Both Jew and Gentile could worship the Lord under David's tent. The tent, known as David's tabernacle, was later replaced by worship in the temple. Davidic worship was embraced and reinstituted by seven subsequent leaders in the history of Israel and Judah.

David, the man after God's heart (Acts 13:22), built a house where God's glory could dwell and where His people could meet with Him. David made intimacy with God the magnificent obsession of his life (Psalm 27:4). David's heart embodies God's desire for humanity in our day. David established a new order of worship as part of his focused efforts to please God. The new order of worship had not been experienced before David's time, but it was God's will for that hour.

God desires to release a new order of worship in the earth that will reform the very fabric of the Church. This order of worship will be new to us but not to God, who spoke through His prophet Amos that God would rebuild David's fallen tent. This new order of worship is part of the roadmap God is releasing to take the body of Christ into unchartered territories of victory.

God is restoring the Tabernacle of David in our day. No more will God's children gather once a week for a few hours, but it will turn into meetings that never end as the children of God encounter the beauty of Lord! Our services will break out into continuous worship and prayer celebrations.

God created the heavens and the earth in His first recorded act in history (Genesis 1:1). In heaven the one true God is acknowledged as Lord of all, receiving the worship He alone deserves (Revelation 4). The one who desired to be like God, satan, was expelled from heaven along with a third of the angels in heaven (Isaiah 14:12-14, Revelation 12:4). God gave stewardship of the earth to man, intending it to be a colony of heaven where man could freely worship Him. Jacob described the house of God at the gateway of heaven (Genesis 28:17). In Matthew 6 Jesus taught His disciples to pray that His Kingdom would come on the earth "as it is in heaven."

The rebuilding of David's Tabernacle—executed through believers' worship and intercession—will be the foundation of God's plan to bring heaven's rule to earth. As David's Tabernacle is restored, the space between heaven and earth will decrease, and cities will become what God intended. Restoring David's Tabernacle will restore Kingdom authority to the children of God. His children will demolish the works of the enemy that have prevented the spread of the knowledge of God in the earth. The spirit of revelation, understanding, and wisdom will be poured out on the people of God as the glory of the Father is unveiled. So too will our hearts burn in this coming season as we see Him as we've never seen Him before (Revelation 4).

The rebuilding of David's Tabernacle will re-establish the foundation of the Church, ushering in a kairos moment in history. God is jealous for His house to be known once again as a house of prayer for all nations. Many saints have already glimpsed what God desires for Planet Earth through visions and dreams, but God must find a people who will partner with Him as co-laborers to see it take place. This is a time of great change in the earth, the hour where God will make all things new as He rebuilds David's fallen tent.

God is shifting the Church from a consumer culture to a Kingdom culture. In a Kingdom culture, the King is the focus of His subjects, and the King delights to provide for His subjects, having all the resources of the Kingdom at His disposal. This is what Jesus alluded to when He declared, "Most assuredly, I say to you, unless you eat the flesh of the Son of Man and drink His blood, you have no life in you" (John 6:53). Jesus was certainly interested in meeting the needs of people, but He had made it clear that the primary goal involved devotion and submission to God. The obedience He required prompted many disciples to walk away from Him (John 6:66), and God is asking His children to rise to a similar challenge today.

The father is challenging the consumer culture because it worships the needs of people rather than the One who can fulfill those needs. We must embrace the culture of the Kingdom where devotion to Jesus is the primary core value.

To build the Kingdom culture in this hour, we must turn our affections toward heaven, and this must be the simple priority of our public gatherings. Our corporate meetings must be marked by divine encounters with the King, and our teaching model must lead people to engagement with God. This environment of intimacy with God will facilitate greater connection and the release of His divine energy into our communities. The early Church experienced life-changing transformation as they pursued God, and these encounters influenced the communities around them as well as their immediate gatherings. The Holy Spirit will release His present word and teach us the multi-varied ways we can experience Him. Worship will not just be about music anymore, but will find expression in the arts, painting, poetry, and drama. The Holy Spirit is beginning to reveal what it will mean to rebuild the Tabernacle of David, bringing a radical change of expression to the Church universal. A new day is dawning for the saints of God!

REBUILDING DAVID'S TABERNACLE: WHAT WILL BE ACCOMPLISHED

1. We will acknowledge our need for God. While He walked the earth Jesus acknowledged His absolute dependence upon the Father. We have the same great privilege of partnering with God to bring about His will on the earth. Now, as it was during Jesus' earthly ministry, nothing shall be impossible to the people of God. We've been created in His image—wired to be in absolute need of Him. As we acknowledge this need, we gain a heavenly perspective and we are seated in heavenly places in Christ. God has provided the means for victory as we keep our hearts and minds fixed heavenward (John 15:5, John 5:19, Colossians 3:2).

2. God will be enthroned in our worship. Through the sacrifice of Jesus on the cross, God gave us the privilege of becoming citizens of heaven (Philippians 3:20). When we worship God, He inhabits and is enthroned in the praises of His children. Our worship and prayer link heaven to earth.

3. The sounds of heaven will be released on earth. God intended for every city and nation on earth to have a unique sound and rhythm. We see this demonstrated when we travel across our country or to different parts of the world. By God's design each culture favors a particular sound and style of music. As we partner with God to rebuild the Tabernacle of David, God will release the sounds of heaven over cities and nations, even as He orchestrates unprecedented revival. Sounds never before heard on earth will turn the darkest hearts back to God and transform nations. God's skilled musicians, His Kingdom sons and daughters, will influence the cultures of continents.

4. The Church will be trained and equipped. God's goal for the Church isn't just to get people born again and gather them in a building a few times a week. His higher goal is for the knowledge of His Son to flood the nations as the waters cover the sea (Habakkuk 2:14). Jesus modeled what He intends for the Church: His disciples walked with Him in intimacy. They were with Him nearly twenty-four hours a day for three years and were empowered with His authority to do the very same work He was doing (Matthew 10:1). In this context of continually beholding the face of God, we build the foundation for true discipleship, empowerment and multiplication. Rebuilding of the Tabernacle of David will change the way believers are equipped for the work of the ministry.

5. A Prophetic Sign: God wants His people to come fully into His purposes and 24/7 worship and prayer is a tangible symbol of His intention—a prophetic sign for humanity in this hour. We are to live in conscious reality of God around the clock.

AS WE PARTNER WITH GOD TO REBUILD THE TABERNACLE OF DAVID, GOD WILL RELEASE THE SOUNDS OF HEAVEN OVER CITIES AND NATIONS, EVEN AS HE ORCHESTRATES UNPRECEDENTED REVIVAL. SOUNDS NEVER BEFORE HEARD ON EARTH WILL TURN THE DARKEST HEARTS BACK TO GOD AND TRANSFORM NATIONS.

WE ARE THE CLEAREST LIKENESS TO GOD ON EARTH. THE GLORY OF GOD IS RESIDENT IN EACH OF US, AND HIS GLORY IS RELEASED WHEN WE CO-LABOR TO EXTEND HIS KINGDOM ON EARTH. WE ARE NOT LITTLE GODS UPON THE EARTH, BUT CHILDREN OF GOD WHO'VE BECOME PARTAKERS OF THE DIVINE NATURE.

CHAPTER FOUR

CO-LABORERS WITH GOD

It's been more than three months since the day life changed irrevocably for John and Diana Robinson and thousands of others in the South Bend region. Many wonderful transformations continue in the lives of those who participate in the revival. The outpouring seems to have picked up the pace of activity in the lives of believers, adding to already hectic schedules, yet people like John and Diana don't seem stressed or tired at all. This is quite a change because in the past John and Diana always seemed to be exhausted, even after having a few days to relax.

On this particular evening John and Diana leave their children home with the baby-sitter before embarking on "date night" to enjoy each other's company at their favorite Italian restaurant. They share the God encounters each of them has had recently, as well as the words of guidance and comfort each of them has heard from God. As the couple finishes their meal, the tangible presence of God seems to hover over their table, and they both recognize that God is leading them to the stadium that night to join many thousands of others who are worshipping there. Few words are spoken as they drive to the stadium, and the couple basks in the warmth of God's presence. This is new and different for John and Diana, who formerly seemed to equate spiritual activity with closeness to God in the past. As they focus on receiving from God, they become much more effective and fruitful in other areas of life.

They arrive at the stadium and quickly locate seats. As John sits down he goes into a deep encounter. John's spirit shoots out of his body, and he ascends high above the stadium into the heavens. John's body is on the earth, but his spirit is high above. He rockets higher and higher when suddenly the brightest light he's ever encountered surrounds him. John's eyes adjust to the brightness when he arrives at a room—surprisingly, a room with his name painted on the wall. The room has pictures from throughout his life, from infancy to adulthood. There are also pictures of him in the future, and John is amazed by the room's beautiful colors. He's almost embarrassed that someone went through such lavish efforts to create a room just for him.

A DIVINE ENCOUNTER

Just then a man appears, standing in front of John. The man has the most beautiful smile, and he extends his hand, saying, "Hi John, my name is Nathaniel. Many of us here have waited excitedly for this moment since the foundation of the earth." John is absolutely stunned, wondering what's taking place and how he ended up in this room. Nathaniel explains that God the Father had intimate knowledge of John before he was even born, and the room was built to unveil the great destiny God has for his life. "John, this room exists in the heart of God for you," Nathaniel says, "and for the entire human race from before the world began." As Nathaniel answers questions, his countenance begins to change. Nathaniel laments that most of humanity has never understood how precious God's thoughts are towards them (Psalm 139:17). "Heaven has waited for this moment in time, when the goodness, beauty, and majesty of King Jesus will be demonstrated to the nations. The Father has longed to extend His mercy and goodness so that the world can know He is the one true and living God. The Father created the earth to contain and reveal His glory. Know and understand, John, that you are living in a strategic hour of unveiling, and the Father has invited you into the council of heaven to exercise your role as a conduit of His glory in the earth."

> "HEAVEN HAS WAITED FOR THIS MOMENT IN TIME, WHEN THE GOODNESS, BEAUTY, AND MAJESTY OF KING JESUS WILL BE DEMONSTRATED TO THE NATIONS. THE FATHER HAS LONGED TO EXTEND HIS MERCY AND GOODNESS SO THAT THE WORLD CAN KNOW HE IS THE ONE TRUE AND LIVING GOD. "

As Nathanial prophesies, the words enter John's heart like rolling thunder, "From this day, My son, you will live with continuous understanding of My goodness and you will hear and know My voice with a clarity you've never known before. When you stand at life's critical crossroads, you will hear My voice and you will understand My purposes during every season of your life." John is once again stunned, recalling his journal entry that morning where he expressed a deep desire to hear the voice of God in a way he'd never known.

As John wonders why God allowed him to see this room, a table and two chairs suddenly appear, and Nathaniel invites John to join him at the table. As John sits down, he observes large book with his name on the cover. Nathaniel instructs him to turn to page 150, where he observes a prayer that he and Diana prayed before going to bed a few weeks earlier. They had prayed for a greater understanding of God's purposes for their lives, even if it came in an unusual way. As John reads the prayer—which he had already forgotten—Nathaniel lovingly reminds John that God the Father hears every prayer His children pray. "Not only does the Father hear every prayer and petition made by His children, He often makes them participants in the answers to their prayers. Often obedience is a necessary requirement to facilitate the encounter. While we never can earn anything in this glorious Kingdom, God has chosen to honor our cooperation and partnership. When you prayed, you positioned yourself to receive the inheritance reserved for you by the Father. In the past you've mocked those who've displayed emotion and claimed unusual experiences with God. Remember, John, God can't honor you with the very thing you've chosen to dishonor. The Father heard your prayer a few weeks ago and responded by moving on the hearts of you and your wife, prompting you to come to the stadium tonight. An angel was stationed at the stadium and helped facilitate the encounter you are now experiencing—he had been ordained to do so from the beginning of time. Your obedience to the Father's voice tonight inclined your heart to receive this encounter, and you will have similar encounters the rest of your life as long as your heart is postured in this way."

Nathaniel goes on to tell of the riches available to every son and daughter of the Kingdom: "The Son of God, through His death on the cross, has linked heaven and earth. All the resources of the Kingdom are available for you to have great success in the earth." The encounter gets better and better, and the revelation of God's majesty reveals how narrow John's view of God has been. John, wondering if Nathanial is an angel, once again receives an answer to his questions.

"Of course I am an angel of God, and we are all sent as ministering spirits." John is amazed that God would reveal Himself to such an ordinary guy, allowing him to dialogue with an angel of the Lord. Sensing John's amazement, Nathanial declares, "Your encounters are birthed from the heart of God. These are often given in proportion to your hunger to receive all heaven has for you."

THE SON OF GOD, THROUGH HIS DEATH ON THE CROSS HAS LINKED HEAVEN AND EARTH. ALL THE RESOURCES OF THE KINGDOM ARE AVAILABLE FOR YOU TO HAVE GREAT SUCCESS IN THE EARTH.

What John understood intellectually for many years he now understands by experience. His reason for existence involves ongoing encounters with the heart of God. Nathaniel instructs John to turn to page 165, which is the beginning of a new chapter. Then John turns to the next page, which appears blank. "Through this encounter God has revealed the pattern of experience that will help you navigate the next season of your life. The Father desires divine partnership with you. If you'll diligently listen and follow His voice, God will empower you to become a releaser of His glory and bless you beyond what you've ever imagined."

Nathaniel then asks John, "Have you realized that you have certain God-given desires?"

"Well, I always thought the desires of my heart were completely self-serving and not very spiritual," says John.

"What if I told you that your deepest desires were born in the heart of God?" Nathanial responds. "The Father requires that we fully submit to His lordship. Once He has our hearts, He desires to partner with us in everything to reveal His glory—even your desire to own and operate a hamburger restaurant that would have franchises all around the world. In the coming months, He's going to provide step-by-step plans to realize your dream of starting your first hamburger restaurant. If you adhere to heaven's pattern, it will be a wonderful reflection of His glory. You'll receive a great deal of attention from many different people, but you must always remember that it was God who endowed you with the power to obtain wealth" (Deuteronomy 8:18).

Suddenly John and Nathaniel are lifted up and out of the room and touch down in a nearby hallway—a hallway with many rooms. Nathaniel explains, "Do you see these rooms, John? These are places in the heart of God reserved for you and your wife. Simple surrender and obedience are the keys to accessing these rooms. There's so much abundance and grace available for you in the heart of God. This is what Jesus meant when He said that in the "Father's house there are many dwelling places" (John 14:2).

John immediately drops back into his body as soon as Nathaniel is finished speaking. Visibly disoriented, John feels the effects of the encounter begin to fade. From Diana's perspective, it appeared that John had been electrocuted while in his seat. Diana might have been disconcerted if she had observed such a dramatic manifestation of the Holy Spirit prior to the outpouring, but these occurrences had become fairly commonplace. The outpouring of the Holy Spirit had redefined what "normal" Christianity was for the couple and untold thousands around the globe. The encounter lasted only forty-five minutes, but to John it seemed like many hours had passed. John smiles, remembering that God created time and that eternity has no clock.

John is exhausted. As he and Diana head home, nearly 5,000 people still in the throes of worship remain scattered around the stadium. The tangible presence of God is still very strong, and John and Diana wonder out loud if the meeting will ever end.

John and Diana get home after midnight, and Diana heads right to bed. John plans on joining her but remembers the advice of his pastor who encouraged everyone to record their experiences by writing them down. He takes a seat in his home office and begins to record the message he received from the angel of the Lord. He senses another wave of the Spirit's presence even as he writes. He senses the Lord is pleased by his diligence to meditate on what he has experienced.

God is revolutionizing John's thinking and preparing him for greater intimacy and encounter. God wants John to view reality the way He sees it. His dream to own a business was God-given. God provides greater insight as John writes, reminding him of Jesus' declaration that His words are Spirit and Life (John 6:63).

John and Diana awake after a few hours of sleep, and John rejoices over all that's taken place and all that God had instructed him to do. Diana comes into full agreement and prophesies in greater detail about all that God has spoken to John. They convene the family that afternoon, informing them of all the wondrous things God is doing and speaking. The children nod along, and the family prays together as one.

John and Diana make adjustments to their lifestyle, with John working less overtime at the plant to spend more time with his children. They also decide to make some changes to their charitable giving and finances. While they've always been faithful givers, they now decide to increase their giving by twenty percent, forgoing some luxury expenses. They also decide to meet and pray as a family each morning. Change is never easy, but John and Diana believe these changes were birthed in the heart of God. They note where they need to make adjustments and then come into agreement, asking

God to empower them to obey what they believe He's requiring of them. God meets with them faithfully each morning as they pray as a family, even if it's only for a few minutes at the start of a busy day. John's encounter has become a doorway to a whole new way of living for the Robinsons.

RELATIONSHIPS THAT PRODUCE

Genesis, the book of origins, provides foundational principles for relating to God. The synergistic relationship of the Triune God worked together as one to create the world. The God who spoke the earth into existence also told His creation to be fruitful and to multiply. He called the land to produce vegetation and trees to bear fruit with seeds (Genesis 1:11). He created the living creatures to increase, produce, and multiply (Genesis 1:22, 24) in order to extend the glory of God throughout the earth. God created man and woman as the crowning achievement of His creation:

> Then God said, "Let Us make man in Our image, according to Our likeness; let them have dominion over the fish of the sea, over the birds of the air, and over the cattle, over all the earth and over every creeping thing that creeps on the earth" (Genesis 1:26).

God called all that He had created "very good." However, it was the human race that was exclusively created in His image. The word *image* is defined as likeness—that which is a pattern, model, or example of something (Gen. 1:26-27[6]; 5:3; 9:6[7]). Whether this likeness is moral, ethical, physical, or natural is not clear.

---

[6] The word defined occurs twice in this verse

[7] I have cited every reference in regard to this lexeme discussed under this definition.

Being made in God's image means that humans share, though imperfectly and finitely, in God's nature. We share in His communicable attributes (life, personality, truth, wisdom, love, holiness, justice), and so have the capacity for spiritual fellowship with Him.[8]

As people made in the image of God, we are designed for dependence upon Him for every facet of our existence. While we were wired to have our deep needs met in Him, God does not force this relationship. He made a sovereign choice to partner with us that was rooted and grounded in love.

We are the clearest likeness to God on earth. The glory of God is resident in each of us, and His glory is released when we co-labor to extend His Kingdom on earth. How God chose to relate to humanity is a great mystery. We are not little gods upon the earth, but children of God who've become partakers of the divine nature (2 Peter 1:4).

> WE ARE THE CLEAREST LIKENESS TO GOD ON EARTH. THE GLORY OF GOD IS RESIDENT IN EACH OF US, AND HIS GLORY IS RELEASED WHEN WE CO-LABOR TO EXTEND HIS KINGDOM ON EARTH.

I have a picture of my father when he was about seven or eight years old. Pictures of my father are rare, since he grew up in a communist nation and escaped without possessions. I was amazed that my dad looked exactly as I did at that age. I am not my father—even though I greatly desire to have my father's character and values. The same is true for every son and daughter of God. We're not little

---

[8] Walvoord, John F.; Zuck, Roy B.; Dallas Theological Seminary: *The Bible Knowledge Commentary: An Exposition of the Scriptures.* Wheaton, IL: Victor Books, 1983-c1985, S. 1:29

gods but those endowed with the potential to reflect and magnify the One we serve.

We are His delegated representatives. The same moment the Triune God created us in His image, He also gave us the clear directive to rule over and subdue the earth (Genesis 1:26). In stewarding the earth, we fulfill part of the reason for our existence.

Leaving a godly mark on the world is very satisfying. All humanity dreams of making significant impact on the world. The earth is to be a place where we leave our imprint for the glory of God. The image of God provides each person with tremendous potential to shape the world. I've always loved going to live sporting events to witness what I consider to be the splendor and majesty of arena and stadium architectural structures. Arenas and stadiums are among the most beautiful structures on earth. I don't know if the architects of most stadiums and arenas were professing believers in Jesus Christ, but I believe they reflect His beauty. These architects used their God-given talents and gifts to create beauty as co-laborers with God in the earth.

History is replete with examples of individuals who stewarded the world and changed the course of history. Some stewarded properly, while others misappropriated their God-given privilege. Those who misappropriated were used by the devil to inflict death, pain, and destruction on others. These evil acts were never God's intention for humanity, but He always honored the volition of humankind, allowing us free will to choose good or evil.

We could all name historical figures that shaped the world in a positive way, perhaps mentioning illustrious personages such as Winston Churchill, Martin Luther, Martin Luther King, Jr., Thomas Edison, and others. Entire libraries are devoted to people who made the world better. A small sampling of those who stewarded the earth well might include the following:

- **Samuel Johnson** wrote the Dictionary of the English Language, published in 1755 after nine years of work. His dictionary has had far-reaching impact on modern English and has been described as "one of the greatest single achievements of scholarship." The dictionary brought Johnson popularity and success. Until the completion of the Oxford English Dictionary 150 years later, Johnson's was viewed as the pre-eminent British dictionary.

- **Edward Jenner**, an English doctor, popularized the smallpox vaccination and became the father of immunology.

- **Dorothy Gerber** invented baby food in 1927.

- **Willis Haviland Carrier** invented the air conditioner in 1902.

- **J. Stuart Blackton** invented animation and motion pictures in 1906.

- **Fritz Pfleumer** invented the audiotape in 1928.

These great reformers changed their fields or created new ones that didn't exist, and knowingly or unknowingly embodied part of God's great desire for humanity. They became ambassadors of God in the world, improving life for all of us on earth.

History's outstanding men and women are only part of the story when it comes to God's divine design for humanity. God wanted the earth to be governed by a prescribed pattern and order. Because we were created in God's image, we were designed to experience great joy through our dependence and co-laboring with Him. We achieve great significance, and God receives great glory as humanity exalts the Creator of heaven and earth through full expression of the glory He placed within us.

As the first human with a commission to rule and steward the earth, God allowed Adam to name every animal. Adam assigned names to every living creature on earth—doing so without God's intervention—and these names have endured throughout history (Genesis 2:19-20). A divine pattern was established for how God desires to relate to humanity. God, who as the creator and source of all things spoke the universe into existence, made a choice to allow Adam to speak and then name the animals.

Is this still God's will for today? How was it possible for Adam to name each animal in the exact way that God intended? Was God's intention supernaturally discerned, or was it birthed through the naming process? Although Scripture may not provide precise answers to all the mysteries of divine partnership, I believe there is significant revelation and insight in Genesis 2:25, "And they were both naked, the man and his wife, and were not ashamed." In the perfection of God's creation, Adam and Eve felt no shame because they thought of each other in the way God intended. Evil, death, and destruction were never God's plan for His creation. God wants to walk and commune with us in the cool of day (Genesis 3:8). He wants to share the desires of His heart so we can steward the earth for His glory. Through union with Him, we are to be God-conscious—to have His mind and heart, and this enables us to be co-laborers with Him.

God assigned Adam the specific role of caretaker in the Garden of Eden, fulfilling God's mandate for humanity to exercise dominion (Genesis 2:15). He was free to eat from all of the trees in the garden except the tree of the knowledge of good and evil. If Adam chose against God's directive, death would result. On the other hand, Adam could choose to subject himself to God's dominion, but the privilege came with responsibility. Adam and Eve's eventual sin subjected humanity to shame, guilt, and separation from God. But God's original intention for humanity remains intact, despite the evil and destruction resulting from the first couple's choice.

The restoration plan for humanity was in God's heart from before the foundation of the earth. Jesus became the Lamb who was slain. The Son of God redeemed us and provided us with an understanding exceeding that of Adam and Eve. God walked with Adam and Eve, but the new covenant empowers Him to dwell *within* us. We are a new race of people upon the earth, releasing the Father's favor and glory.

The Word who became flesh, Jesus Christ, modeled the life that the Father desires for each of His sons and daughters. Jesus, who was fully God and fully man, emptied Himself of His divinity (Philippians 2) and lived as man in complete dependence on the Father, providing us with a pattern. His dependency allowed Him to see life from the Father's perspective (John 5:19-20). When others saw ignorant and unlearned fishermen, Jesus saw Apostles of the Lamb who would turn the world upside down (Acts 4:13-17:6). When there were only two loaves and five fishes to feed 5,000, Jesus took it as a down payment and multiplied it to meet the need

WE WERE DESIGNED TO EXPERIENCE GREAT JOY THROUGH OUR DEPENDENCE AND CO-LABORING WITH HIM. WE ACHIEVE GREAT SIGNIFICANCE, AND GOD RECEIVES GREAT GLORY AS HUMANITY EXALTS THE CREATOR OF HEAVEN AND EARTH THROUGH FULL EXPRESSION OF THE GLORY HE PLACED WITHIN US.

(John 6:1-15). While others grieved the death of His friend Lazarus, Jesus saw it as an opportunity for God to be glorified (John 11). All who believe in His name have the opportunity to see things from the Father's perspective and to live with a God-consciousness. God is redefining what it means to represent Him. When God created Adam, He could have given him a detailed list for personal development, perhaps including things like developing a strong prayer life, building a nice building where you can meet with God, and learning to evangelize effectively.

While all are excellent suggestions, God specifically charged Adam with caretaking responsibilities of the Garden of Eden (Genesis 2:15). God's choice for Adam's occupation was profound, making no distinction between the secular and sacred. The whole earth was meant to reflect His glory. Adam's stewardship of the garden demonstrates God's greater purpose for all humanity: to reflect His glory in everything we do—in every task, however mundane.

Considerable debate rages within the body of Christ about the foremost priority of the Church, centered on where we should be spending the bulk of our time, energy and resources. Is it to simply get people saved, or to get them saved and also work for social justice? While these are valid questions, they are not options found in Scripture. The heart of God is for man to become a new creation and be restored back to wholeness, His original intention found in the Garden of Eden. This is the gospel of the Kingdom that Jesus preached. God is giving us the gift of His mindset—the ability to think and see things as He sees them—so that everything we touch will be marked by the wisdom of our Father in heaven. The Apostle Paul plumbs this profound mystery in 1 Corinthians 2:16, "For 'who has known the mind of the Lord that he may instruct Him?' But we have the mind of Christ." Our ability to represent the Father

> GOD IS GIVING US THE GIFT OF HIS MINDSET—THE ABILITY
> TO THINK AND SEE THINGS AS HE SEES THEM—SO THAT
> EVERYTHING WE TOUCH WILL BE MARKED BY THE WISDOM OF
> OUR FATHER IN HEAVEN.

begins by allowing His operating system, His mind, to become our own. The following scriptural principles facilitate that transformation.

INTENTIONALITY WITH GOD'S RESOURCES

God has given us access to an abundance of resources that we can only receive through intentionality. In the Gospels, Jesus asks a number of people in obvious need if they want a miracle (John 5:1-17, Mark 10:46-52). Jesus wasn't trying to be cruel. He wanted people to understand how He thinks. When we think like Him, we live like Him. The miraculous or supernatural dimension is not designed for temporary relief or for the miracle someone needs in the moment. Miracles are an invitation to view reality differently. Jesus preached repentance—a call to change the way we think. Embracing the Kingdom of Heaven requires us to think like God (Matthew 4:17). The Judaism of the Pharisees was structured to hasten the Kingdom of God. However, it was a religious system with the right goal but the wrong roadmap. In this hour, God is once again challenging the Church to examine our current goals and roadmaps. Intentionality gives God permission to challenge our thought processes. As the Apostle Paul admonishes in Romans 12:1-2, "I beseech you therefore, brethren, by the mercies of God, that you present your bodies a living sacrifice, holy, acceptable to

God, *which is* your reasonable service. And do not be conformed to this world, but be transformed by the renewing of your mind, that you may prove what *is* that good and acceptable and perfect will of God."

INTENTIONALITY FOCUSES OUR AFFECTIONS

Intention is a specific choice we make by the grace of God to set our affections on God. When we intentionally focus our hearts and affections on Him, it transforms the way we think (Proverbs 23:7). What we treasure most in our hearts will command our attention (Matthew 6:21). Our hearts are the center of our spiritual lives—the seat of our thoughts, passions, desires, appetites, affections, purposes, endeavors.[9] The affections of our heart determine our thoughts, which in turn give birth to our attitudes and actions.

INTENTIONALLY ENCOUNTERING GOD

If we live intentionally, our focus is not on our failings but rather on the One who can never fail. Moses was intentional in turning aside to see the burning bush, and it is clear that God wanted to change Moses' understanding of his life through this encounter. This one divine encounter was not unto perfection, but was part of God's divine design to shift Moses' view of reality (Exodus 3). The Father desires divine encounter with us on a continual basis, allowing His children to see themselves in light of who He is and His eternal purposes for our lives. The Apostle Paul put this concept into words when he wrote in 2 Corinthians 3:18, "But we all, with

---

[9] Strong, J. 1996. *The exhaustive concordance of the Bible: Showing every word of the test of the common English version of the canonical books, and every occurrence of each word in regular order.* (electronic ed.). Woodside Bible Fellowship, Ontario

unveiled face, beholding as in a mirror the glory of the Lord, are being transformed into the same image from glory to glory, just as by the Spirit of the Lord."

God doesn't simply express glory, He *is* glory—and this glory resides in every one of His sons and daughters. Heaven's desire, as described by the Apostle Paul, is for our experience to become more and more glorious with each successive encounter, even as the Holy Spirit equips us to more fully experience all the Father has made available. This process transforms the way we think.

The Apostle Paul's conversion experience is a prime example of how divine encounter can dramatically change our view of reality. Acts 9 says Paul (called Saul before his conversion) was "breathing murderous threats against the Lord's disciples," but when Paul encountered Jesus on the road to Damascus and heard the Lord's voice, he was immediately converted. The Book of Acts is Luke's effort to chronicle all of Paul's ministry exploits. In his teachings and in defense of those teachings, Paul invokes his encounter experience with Jesus on the road to Damascus again and again, calling it the encounter that changed his reality and destiny.

The touchstone of the transformed mind is change in how we think. The word *think* is defined as: having a conscious mind, to some extent of reasoning, remembering experiences, and making rational decisions. Our thoughts are transformed through encounter with our Father's heavenly reality.

We should confront the obstacles and mountains of life in the light of revelation we receive from Him. Our Father is never shaken or taken aback by our circumstances. He knows the beginning from the end (Revelation 22:13). We were designed to navigate life through the lens of deep and ongoing encounter with Him.

A number of years ago, I was cleaning my house and worshipping God when I heard the Holy Spirit speak clearly, "Abner, you know that problems and difficulties are just an opportunity for Me to show My goodness." I remember rejoicing over this great word the Father gave me and thinking how I was going to share it at my next speaking event. A few days later, however, two teenagers broke into the small office in my home and stole my most valuable items, including my laptop, which seemed to have my entire life on it. I realized the Father was graciously allowing me to experience difficulty in light of the revelation that I received from Him.

TRUTH TO DEVELOP THE TRANSFORMED MIND

Jesus declared Himself to be "the way, the truth, and the life" (John 14:6). Jesus, the God-Man, desires to be known. He calls us to encounter as a way of life. Speaking to the Jews who believed in Him, Jesus said that they would know truth, and the truth would set them free. They gained knowledge of the truth through intimate personal experience with Jesus (John 8:31-32). This is why James admonishes us to draw near to God.

A lack of understanding of who God is often limits our ability to appropriate the resources He has made available. False conceptions about His character often become self-fulfilling prophecies in the lives of believers. For example, a man works eighty hours a week, believing that is the only way he can survive financially. This false idea he's chosen to believe limits how God is going to provide for him, in effect keeping God's goodness and mercy at arm's length. God can certainly provide for this man or anyone else regardless, but it is unlikely, given this belief that there is the only avenue by which God will provide. Quite often, what we believe about God's nature determines how much of His provision we can receive.

Jesus yearns to remove every false concept. Through divine encounter He will reveal these misconceptions e.g., anything that limits our ability to become imitators of Him on earth.

A LACK OF UNDERSTANDING OF WHO GOD IS FOR US OFTEN LIMITS OUR ABILITY TO APPROPRIATE THE RESOURCES HE HAS MADE AVAILABLE. FALSE CONCEPTIONS ABOUT HIS CHARACTER OFTEN BECOME SELF-FULFILLING PROPHECIES IN THE LIVES OF BELIEVERS.

TRANSFORMATION THROUGH THE WORD.

The Father chooses to speak to His children through multiple channels, including dreams, visions, and other people, but the word of God defines our boundaries. Jesus declared, "Men shall not live by bread alone but by every word that proceeds from the mouth of God" (Matthew 4:4). Hebrews 4:12 says, "The word of God is living and powerful, and sharper than any two-edged sword, piercing even to the division of soul and spirit, and of joints and marrow, and is a discerner of the thoughts and intents of the heart." God speaks to us through His word, searching our motives and enriching our understanding. Like a plumb line, the word helps us see where we are in relation to what He wants us to be. The word of God frees us of from the entanglements of wrong thinking and invites us to upgrade our thoughts through divine encounter.

THE SPIRIT OF REVELATION

The spirit of revelation is listed among the seven spirits of God that play a distinctive role in the development of the transformed mind (Isaiah 11:1, Revelation 4:5). Revelation can be defined as un-covering or disclosing. The gift of prophecy is an incredible example of the spirit of revelation in operation. A prophetic word reveals the truth about a person, local assembly, city, or region. The prophetic word, which has been on God's mind from the beginning of time, is now revealed to humankind. The spirit of revelation is ever at work during encounters with God. God wants us to live not only by His principles but also by revelation.

For example, let's say you experienced a breakthrough in your prayers for healing. Someone was healed of deafness last week be-cause you anointed the person's ears with oil before engaging in prayer. If you pray for a deaf person again this week you might anoint the person's ears again since that was how you received your breakthrough last week. But this time God may choose to heal in a completely different manner. When we live in the spirit of revela-tion, we invite God's thoughts into specific situations. This enables a living, vibrant relationship with Him.

Revelation knowledge is not the same as intellectual comprehen-sion:

- The spirit of revelation may be at odds with your intellectual instincts.

- Biblically, revelation denotes experience, emotion, and per-sonal relationship.

- Every revelation allows us to draw nearer to God through our inquiries of Him.

- Revelation knowledge may not be fully understood in the moment.

- The spirit of revelation is critical to our life of faith. The Apostle Paul prayed, "I do not cease to give thanks for you, making mention of you in my prayers: that the God of our Lord Jesus Christ, the Father of glory, may give to you the spirit of wisdom and revelation in the knowledge of Him" (Ephesians 1:16-17).

FAITH

The spirit of revelation must be exercised through wisdom and faith. When the Father speaks and reveals, He does so from a different reality than ours. In visitations to men and women throughout Scripture, God often reveals that His purposes are at cross-purposes with theirs. We could cite Moses, Gideon, Mary, and Saul, just to name a few. But we grab hold of revelation by exercising our faith. Faith is the application of revelation and it is so critical because it's impossible to please God without it (Hebrews 11:6). Consider the story of Abraham: "And not being weak in faith, he [Abraham] did not consider his own body, already dead (since he was about a hundred years old), and the deadness of Sarah's womb. He did not waver at the promise of God through unbelief, but was strengthened in faith, giving glory to God" (Romans 4:19-20).

SPEAKING AND DECLARING

The words we speak were once thoughts treasured in our hearts. Speaking and declaring are critical components to manifesting the will of God in the earth. The God who spoke the universe into existence now allows us to use the medium of speech to help create the realities of heaven here on earth. If we align with God's thinking, our words reflect the rhythms of heaven. Worship and thanksgiving empower us to speak in rhythm with the language of heaven. We are to give thanks in every situation because praise and thanksgiving create faith in our hearts and minds for what God will bring to pass (1 Thessalonians 5:18).

> THE GOD WHO SPOKE THE UNIVERSE INTO EXISTENCE NOW ALLOWS US TO USE THE MEDIUM OF SPEECH TO HELP CREATE THE REALITIES OF HEAVEN HERE ON EARTH. IF WE ALIGN WITH GOD'S THINKING, OUR WORDS REFLECT THE RHYTHMS OF HEAVEN.

LIVING WITH GOD-CONSCIOUSNESS

To inherit the Kingdom of God, we must learn to be God-conscious, keeping our hearts and minds fixed on Him. Invite the Holy Spirit, the third Person of the Trinity, into every aspect of your life. He's not merely interested in sharing our devotional time—He wants us to share our lives with Him! As children of God we must diligently invite Him into every activity and decision of our lives. God operates differently than the world. After inviting God into our lives, we soon recognize that His ways do not adhere to that of the worldly system. The heavenly mindset carries the absolute conviction that what we experience in God is greater than that which is contrary to His will on earth. The wisdom of heaven may appear to be illogical at times and may not make sense to us. It seemed illogical when Samuel anointed David to be the next King of Israel, but David was God's choice (1 Samuel 16).

THE ISSUE OF OBEDIENCE IS SETTLED

God desires His sons and daughters to obey quickly when He speaks. Obedience to the Father allows heaven to invade our circumstances, establishing His lordship. While the Father relates to us as sons and daughters, Jesus expressed a desire to relate to us as friends. Jesus defined His friends as those willing to obey His commandments. God desires our individual obedience to create a domino effect on the world around us. David's obedience to God allowed him to prepare materials that would be included in the temple that his son Solomon would construct (2 Chronicles 5:1). Jesus' obedience to His Father turned water into wine and inspired the disciples to believe He was the Messiah (John 2:11). Obedience is also a key that positions us for greater visitation (John 14:23). Obedience is a settled issue for those who desire to have the mind of Christ.

Children of God do not *try* to be victorious. We live in vital connection to the victorious King of heaven. Jesus never promised a life free of difficulty; rather, He encourages us to rejoice over the fact that He's overcome every difficulty (John 16:33). To walk in victory we must only meditate on what He has spoken. As a former collegiate wrestler, I learned that practice was an essential part of winning. A regulation collegiate match lasts only seven minutes, but my teammates and I prepared for hours to be victorious because there's no time to "think" about my reaction to my opponent during a match. Similarly, one of the goals of biblical meditation is to train our reactions to situations ahead of time. We don't deny the existence of contrary thoughts and experiences—we simply confront them from God's perspective (2 Corinthians 10:3-5).

It violates our identity as sons and daughters to meditate on thoughts or circumstances contrary to the heart of God for our lives. Victory is assured, but we must have courage to stand on the promises of God in the midst of great adversity, just as Joshua did. Victory comes as we defeat adversity, and so we embrace adversity as an opportunity to walk out the victory God has already promised.

> Only be strong and very courageous, that you may observe to do according to all the law which Moses My servant commanded you; do not turn from it to the right hand or to the left, that you may prosper wherever you go. This Book of the Law shall not depart from your mouth, but you shall meditate in it day and night, that you may observe to do according to all that is written in it. For then you will make your way prosperous, and then you will have good success (Joshua 1:6-8).

God has provided a strategic tool that enables us to pray the perfect will of God at all times and in every circumstance: the gift of tongues (Acts 2:38). The gift of tongues is not one-dimensional; there are tongues of men and tongues of angels, and through them God has provided a way that we can pray as He intends (1 Corinthians 13:1).

> For we do not know what we should pray for as we ought, but the Spirit Himself makes intercession for us with groanings which cannot be uttered (Romans 8:26).

Crises engulf many nations of the earth, and our world is in desperate need of hope. God wants His Church to be a shining beacon of hope to a world that is lost without Him. The blood of Jesus has restored us as stewards of the earth—God's original intention for us.

He is calling us to transform our minds to reflect His thoughts and, through union with Him, impact nations.

God's reformers and agents of change will touch every sphere of society. Reformers in the arts and entertainment will create films, paintings, songs, and dance birthed from the heart of the Father for world influence. Reformers in government will herald the lordship of Jesus in their workplaces, creating communities where all can achieve greatness. Reformers in education will implement principles that will gain worldwide acclaim. It is indeed a kairos moment. All the resources of the Kingdom are available to those who discern the Father's heart in this hour.

IT IS INDEED A KAIROS MOMENT. ALL THE RESOURCES OF THE KINGDOM ARE AVAILABLE TO THOSE WHO DISCERN THE FATHER'S HEART IN THIS HOUR.

GOD GAVE HIS CHURCH MANY GIFTS TO MAKE IT VICTORIOUS AND RELEVANT IN THE WORLD. WE CAN ONLY BE RELEVANT, IF WE EXERCISE THE GIFTS HE ORDAINED AND THE TOOLS HE PROVIDED TO BUILD HIS CHURCH.

CHAPTER FIVE

SIGNS, WONDERS, AND MIRACLES

The "24/7" meetings that marked the initial outpour-ing of the Holy Spirit have continued at Notre Dame Stadium. About one-third of the seats are occupied on most nights, but the stadium is filled to capacity this Thursday evening. The atmosphere is pregnant with expectancy because the Holy Spirit visitation has taken a dramatic turn, increasing in intensity like a tropical storm that suddenly morphs into a hurricane. Throughout the week the Lord's presence has come with ever-increasing intensity, undulating through the crowd like ocean waves, then crashing over the people like breakers on the shore.

Last Thursday the glory of the Lord hovered over the stadium like a beautiful blue cloud. Those in attendance could only watch in silent wonder. Atop the blue spectacle, a fire appeared to be burning, even as the presence of the Lord engulfed and settled on the people. It was like the description in the Book of Acts, where tongues of fire rested on those who were gathered. Many were profoundly touched by the power of God. It was as if an electrical current had passed through their bodies. The worship team lay scattered across the stage like driftwood, some continuing to minister in song from their knees, while others lay prostrate or flat on their backs, singing to the Lord.

An impartation of power accompanied the cloud, and unusual signs and wonders manifested throughout the stadium. Jim and Marlene Dowd were in attendance when the cloud first appeared. Jim was healed instantly from lower back pain that had prevented him from working for the past fifteen years. Marlene was also instantly healed of pain in her left shoulder that for seven years had often prevented her from lifting her hands in worship. Robert Johnson, a regular at the stadium meetings, described a feeling of warmth that penetrated his forehead until both of his blind eyes were opened and healed. Since then, Robert has been reading his Bible without Braille for the first time in fifteen years. Juanita Berry, a woman deaf in her left ear, also experienced the power of God. While worshipping the Lord, she suddenly heard her left ear pop and was completely healed.

The words of Jesus, "With God all things are possible" (Matthew 19:26), had become a living reality. Just three days ago, a young woman lost her husband in a car accident, and he was pronounced dead at the scene. Without hesitation she asked medical personnel if she could have the body brought to the stadium. Taken aback, the medical officials were understandably leery but relented, not wanting to upset the widow any further. They carried the corpse into the stadium, and within a few moments the young man's life miraculously returned as he suddenly gasped for breath. No one had prayed over the corpse—the lifeless body was simply ushered into the presence of Lord, and the man who had died out of God's time was suddenly alive and well. Every miracle recorded in the Bible seems to be taking place: the lame walk, the blind see, and the good news of the Kingdom of God is preached throughout the region. Doctors have even advised patients with terminal illnesses to attend the meetings as a first order of treatment—prompted by the sheer volume of verified miracles.

As news of the miracles spreads across the region, believers and unbelievers converge on the meetings en masse. The stadium quickly fills to capacity, but that hasn't stopped thousands of others from gathering outside, trying to get as close as possible. Live webcasts enable thousands around the globe to participate in the continuous meetings virtually. Hotels within a seventy-five mile radius fill to capacity, and flights to South Bend now sell out weeks in advance. The leaders of this move of God have decided to give priority of place to those who are terminally ill and to their families. But the demand is great. Many others who want to be healed try to get as close to the stadium as possible, but the traffic is snarled and seems to get denser all the time.

City officials met with movement leaders recently, trying to make sense of all the logistical issues the gatherings have caused. The leaders decided to ask participants inside the stadium to leave after three hours to make room for the thousands waiting outside to get in. Some local pastors will also use their buildings as satellite locations. These sanctuaries will feature a live webcast of the stadium service, and prayer will be offered for the sick and for those in need of healing. The harvest has indeed been plentiful (Matthew 9:37).

Before this move of God, it never occurred to John that ordinary believers could pray for the sick. Of course, it was possible for certain "special" leaders to pray for the sick and for missionaries in distant places to do so since, to John's way of thinking, these were people who needed that stuff. John and Diana's congregation, South Bend Community Church, has become a satellite campus, and when the call came to recruit volunteers for the healing team, John knew immediately that he was supposed to join.

John is nervous as he joins the healing team informational meeting the first night. The healing team leader has assigned a partner to each member of the team, much the same way Jesus sent His disciples in groups of two to pray for the sick (Mark 6:7). John is relieved to know that he won't have to minister alone. John, a fairly conservative man in his mid-thirties, will work with a young man named Ralph, who happens to have tattoos all over his body along with some prominent piercings. But the seemingly odd pairing doesn't seem to register with Ralph, who is clearly excited about praying for the sick.

"Hi John, I'm Ralph. Are you ready to see some miracles tonight?" John is taken aback by Ralph's boldness and confidence but is also pleased. He reasons that at least half of their team believes there will be miracles taking place tonight.

The church converted the family life center into a healing room, and the healing team stands at the front of the room awaiting those who need prayer. The atmosphere in the room is incredibly peaceful. Live worship from the stadium streams softly through the room's overhead speakers.

The first person to approach John and Ralph is a man in his mid-forties with a neck brace and a noticeable limp. As the man limps forward for prayer Ralph extends his right hand and yells, "You foul spirit of infirmity, let this man go in the name of Jesus!" As soon as the command is issued, the man collapses to the floor in a heap, screaming in a high-pitched voice.

Unfazed, John responds by repeating the command: "You foul spirit of infirmity, let this man go in the name of Jesus!" Ralph instructs John to place his hands on the man's forehead. After a few more moments of prayer, Ralph encourages the man and helps him to his feet. The man takes a few steps, striding forward without the pronounced limp. Ralph encourages the man to take off his neck brace, and the man does so, moving his neck from side to side without pain. Tears stream down the man's face. This is the first time he has been without pain since a car accident ten years ago. Tears of joy cover John's face as well—he is overwhelmed by the goodness of the Father.

Having seen one incredible miracle, John begins to believe the Father's will is to heal every person that comes for prayer. Over the next hour and a half, John and Ralph work as team, praying for a woman with diabetes, a young man in a wheelchair, an elderly lady dying of cancer, and a teenaged girl suffering from a skin disease. Ralph has more experience praying for the sick, and John is more than happy to follow his lead. Each person prayed for testifies some form of healing.

As the ministry time ends, John realizes he's seen the power of God operating to heal the sick for the first time in his life. Jesus was a miracle worker—John always knew that, but he never imagined his own hands would be used as instruments of healing. He treasures these times of divine breakthrough and asks for grace to implement the necessary changes. Ralph is also moved to take his relationship with the Lord to deeper level and pauses to make a decision before leaving the prayer room. While some unanswered questions remain, he nevertheless purposes in his heart to pursue a life of miracles from that day forward.

John thanks Ralph for being such an amazing partner. "Ralph, I noticed that you seemed to know how to minister differently to each person God brought to us tonight."

"Well John, it's pretty simple. God lives inside us, and He who created the universe knows exactly what each person needs. We just need to listen to what He is saying and become His agent of healing."

"Well that makes perfect sense," John responds. "I also noticed your confidence that miracles were going to take place tonight—why is that?"

"Well, John, I was living on the streets with little hope of a future less than two years ago. One cold night, a man and his wife cared enough to reach out to me and share a message about Jesus. They also demonstrated the message by inviting me to live in their home. I've been with them ever since. I took a year to attend our church's school of ministry where we were taught how to hear the voice of the Father and how to pray for the sick and cast out devils. I've had the privilege of praying for hundreds of people who needed healing, some from minor ailments and some who needed an immediate miracle because their life was in danger. Not every person I prayed for was healed, but I witnessed the power of God on many occasions. John, I know this may sound arrogant, but I'm firmly convinced that God wants to heal every sick person with whom we come into contact."

Ralph's amazing story excites and motivates John. He's also intrigued to learn about schools that offer instruction in how to pray for the sick. John naturally assumes that Ralph is in full-time ministry or is being trained for full-time ministry since God is using him so powerfully: "So Ralph, are you planning on going into full-time ministry?"

"No," Ralph responds, "I'm working at Wal-Mart and I believe God is going to give me great favor there to be a voice of influence in the marketplace.

John is taken aback for a few moments. "Ralph, you are so gifted. You seem to have a call to full-time ministry."

"I do indeed," Ralph says with a laugh. "It's my career at Wal-Mart. I see signs and wonders every day while I'm working— there's no separation between my faith and my assignment at Wal-Mart. And speaking of work, John, I have to head there now. It was really great getting to know you, and I look forward to ministering with you again soon." With that, Ralph heads for the door and John realizes that he too should be heading for home.

As John drives home he experiences the same feeling he and Diana had many times during the past weeks—absolute awe at God. But this time John also feels a need to make up for lost time. Although he and Diana have been Christians for many years, it seems they are only now discovering who God is and what He really thinks about them. John is once again struck with eternity. He doesn't want to waste another moment with futile Christian activity, but his deepest desire is now to utilize every moment he has left in this life to give everything to God.

John hears the Holy Spirit speak to his heart, "John, I long to redeem your life and redeem this time for My people. I long to stamp My people with eternity so they might accomplish in a moment what took previous generations many years to build." John has grown to enjoy communing with the Holy Spirit, and he listens attentively when he receives the Spirit's prompting about a Muslim family who reside two houses down the street. "John, it's time for you to minister to them—not in word only, but with power."

John arrives home excited to tell Diana about all he's seen and heard this evening, and Diana is so inspired by the accounts that she also commits to joining the healing team. While the couple has always had a strong marriage, their relationship has become much stronger during the past couple of weeks. Revelation has increased their identity in the Father and oneness before God as a couple.

John is working around the house a few days later when he sees Mr. Akal, his Muslim neighbor, relaxing on the front porch. Their relationship has always been cordial, but John knows little about Mr. Akal's family, even though they've lived a few doors down for more than three years.

John waves to Mr. Akal and, without thinking, hears the words come out of his mouth, "Hello Mr. Akal. I would love to come over and spend time with you and your family today. Would that be OK?" Never one to invite himself to other people's homes, it seems to John as if the words spoke themselves.

To his surprise, Mr. Akal responds, "Sure, John, why don't you come right over!"

When John arrives Mr. Akal leans back in his chair and invites him to sit down. "John, you're not going to believe this," he begins, "but a few nights ago, I had a dream. In this dream a man appeared and told me I was to have you come to my home to give me the words of life that would bring healing to my family. I'm not given to having many dreams, but something in my heart told me this was from God. I was determined, however, if you were supposed to come to my home, that you would be the one to initiate the invitation. So John, thank you for inviting yourself over, and welcome to our home."

Mr. Akal's wife and son soon join them in the living room. Aatif, their son, arrives in a wheelchair because he cannot walk. He is twenty-one and has never walked a day in his life. The Akals are very gracious but John senses they are waiting for him to share the reason for his visit. The moment is God-ordained and John seizes it, asking God to fill him with the words of life.

John launches out nervously, sharing an experience he had as a young man at youth camp where a Baptist evangelist preached a message that revolutionized his life. The evangelist said Jesus Christ was the Son of God who walked the earth and lived a sinless and perfect life. At the conclusion of His life, Jesus died for the sins of humanity and paid the price for all of our sins. "All of us have sinned and all of us are need of Savior… His name is Jesus Christ. I realize you and your family are of the Muslim faith, Mr. Akal, and I'm sure you're sincere in what you believe. But Jesus Christ is the only way to heaven, and only He has the words of life. He is the reason God has brought me to your home. Would each of you like to accept Jesus' sacrifice on the cross?" John asks, looking at Mr. Akal with earnest anticipation.

Mr. Akal responds: "You know, John, I'm sure you really believe in the message you've just shared with us. My family and I are people who try to do our best. I talk to God every day about my son—I ask God if I could take his place, and if He'd let me, I surely would. I'm not sure what I or my wife did that God would not allow my son to be able to walk his entire life."

John is a little stunned. He assumed that his testimony would have inspired the Akal family to surrender their lives to God right on the spot, especially given the divinely-orchestrated events leading him to visit the their home. John explains that God did not put this disease on their son. "Mr. Akal, it is the goodness of God that causes men and women to turn to Him. It's the goodness of God that brought me to your home to tell you about Jesus Christ and give your family a chance to believe in Him."

Mr. Akal, responding to this second plea for salvation, answers, "I appreciate the passion with which you believe in your God. I know I already told you this, but I ask God to allow me to take my son's place in the wheelchair every day. I should also confess that, while I try my best, I know I have done many things that upset God. But still, perhaps my son could have been spared."

John can see the Akals are not ready to receive Jesus Christ but suddenly realizes that perhaps seeing a demonstration of His power will cause them to come to saving faith. He asks the Akals if he can pray for Aatif, and a new boldness and confidence surges through John's body as he walks over to the young man. He asks the Holy Spirit to come, and then commands life to come into Aatif's legs and the nerve signals to go from his brain down to his legs.

After a few moments of declaring God's healing, John ask Aatif if any change has occurred and if he would like to try to walk. Aatif pushes himself out of the wheelchair and tries to take a few steps, but to no avail. No change has taken place despite John's prayers. If he hadn't known it before, John now recognizes his absolute need for God. Whispering quietly to himself, John asks, "God, what should I do now?" The only thought that comes to John's mind is to wash Aatif's feet and then pray for him again.

John asks Mrs. Akal for a towel, water, and basin to wash her son's feet. The Akals hardly know what to make of John's prayers and this odd request. But the love John has for their paralyzed son is clear to see, and they bring the items to John. John begins the task of washing Aatif's feet when he hears the voice of the Holy Spirit say, "John, if you will lay down your life for people, I will do what I am about to do over and over again in your life." John finishes washing Aatif's feet, somewhat startled and not fully comprehending what he just heard from the Holy Spirit.

BESIDE THEMSELVES WITH JOY, AATIF'S PARENTS WEEP AS THEY OBSERVE THEIR BELOVED SON WALKING FOR THE VERY FIRST TIME. MR. AKAL TURNS TO JOHN, "YOU HAVE SHOWN US THAT YOUR GOD IS THE ONE TRUE, LIVING GOD. WE ARE NOW READY TO ACCEPT YOUR GOD AS OUR GOD."

John knows he has reached a decisive moment. The God he serves will demonstrate His power or John will look like a fool. In truth, John isn't sure a miracle is going to take place, but he places his hands on Aatif's forehead and neck in obedience, declaring, "In the name of Jesus Christ be made whole!" He then asks Aatif to stand up and to try to take some steps. Aatif totters and staggers forward awkwardly, trying to gain his balance. But then, to the amazement of all, Aatif begins to walk. Like a toddler taking his first steps, Aatif holds onto John's hands as he moves forward under his own power for the first time in his life.

As the miracle unfolds, the atmosphere of the room shifts, something John has often felt at the stadium. Beside themselves with joy, Aatif's parents weep as they observe their beloved son walking for the very first time. Mr. Akal grabs his video camera to record this event and turns to John, "Mr. Robinson, you have shown us that your God is the one true, living God. We are now ready to accept your God as our God. You've proven that your God is greater than any other. We will surrender our lives joyfully to a God who not only hears, but who also answers prayer."

John is awe-struck by what has happened. It's as though he needs to pinch himself to make sure it's real. John and the Akals grab hands to form a circle as John leads them in a prayer of salvation.

In a moment of time through a demonstration of power, an entire family has been born again and brought into the Kingdom of God.

THE ESSENTIAL ELEMENT OF POWER

Our existence as believers is founded on God's supernatural acts. If we believe in Jesus Christ, we believe in His Father, who spoke the universe into existence. We believe this God has a Son who is fully God and fully man, who was conceived by the third Person of the Trinity inside a teenaged girl named Mary. Jesus, the God-Man, willingly placed Himself under the limitations of humanity.

Jesus was a fascinating child who worked as a carpenter as a young man. He was the first and only human being to live a sinless life. Not until the final three and a half years of His life did He reveal Himself as the promised Messiah to God's chosen people, the nation of Israel. He taught with authority and performed miracles the world had never seen. Jesus performed so many miracles that the Gospel writer John asserted that all the books ever written would not be large enough to record them all (John 22:25). Jesus was crucified for the sins of humanity and was resurrected from the dead on the third day. He then appeared to His disciples, breathed the Holy Spirit on them and promised an empowerment to do the same works He had done. He ascended into heaven and promised to return again for His Church.

This origin story of the Church is full of supernatural activity that must be accepted if we are to believe what God has said about Himself. This launching platform for the Church of Jesus Christ is profoundly indicative of the identity God intends for us in the fabric of our being.

God gave His church many gifts to make it victorious and relevant in the world. We can only be relevant, if we exercise the gifts He ordained and the tools He provided to build His Church. The Apostle Paul articulates this in his letter to the Corinthians,

And God has appointed these in the church: first apostles, second prophets, third teachers, after that miracles, then gifts of healings, helps, administrations, varieties of tongues (1 Corinthians 12:28).

Let me be clear. If a church community does not demonstrate God's power through the gift of miracles and healings, then they are failing to fully utilize the gifts God has already given to His Church. They will only partially represent Him to a world desperately in need of supernatural intervention. Partial representation creates a tremendous vacuum in the world. Jesus defeated hell, death, and the power of sin in order to give the keys of the Kingdom to His Church. These keys give us access to the power and authority necessary to steward the world in which we live. By failing to utilize everything God ordained for the Church, we fail to fully impact our world as God intended. Worse yet, we create confusion about the nature of God. If we can't back up what we preach with power and demonstration, we misrepresent the God we claim to serve.

IF A CHURCH COMMUNITY DOES NOT DEMONSTRATE GOD'S POWER THROUGH THE GIFT OF MIRACLES AND HEALINGS, THEY WILL ONLY PARTIALLY REPRESENT HIM TO A WORLD DESPERATELY IN NEED OF SUPERNATURAL INTERVENTION.

This was never God's intention for the Church. God wants to manifest His wisdom and wonders before every power and principality. The Apostle declares as much in his letter to the Church at Ephesus:

To the intent that now the manifold wisdom of might be made known by the church to the principalities and powers in the heavenly places (Ephesians 3:10).

The word *manifold* used by the Apostle Paul can refer to the beauty of an embroidered pattern or the variety of color in flowers. The manifold wisdom refers to the new relationship between believing Jews and Gentiles in one body. The medium by which this wisdom is communicated is the Church; the recipients are the angelic hosts "in the heavenly realms" (cf. Ephesians 1:3). Principalities and powers are demonic structures that oppose the Church and Good News of the Gospel. Each one of us is significant. Together we make up the community of people known as the Church. Every believer is unique and beautiful in God's sight, representing a different aspect of the manifold wisdom of God when our lives are operating in proper alignment with heaven (1 Peter 4:10). As we express this wisdom of God, we will expose all that stands in opposition to the Lord. Our obedience will help overthrow demonic powers and establish the Kingdom of God. God desires to build a Church with gifts of healings and miracles to destroy darkness and restore the earth. Miracles are an essential tool to help us steward the earth as God intended.

When we invite people to embrace the good news, we must use the same paradigm Jesus used when He walked the earth. Jesus delivered both a message and a demonstration of the Kingdom. When recruiting His disciples, Peter, James, and John, Jesus met them at the point of their need (Luke 5:1-11). The calling of these three disciples, who later became apostles, is just one example of the way Jesus used the resources of heaven to penetrate natural circumstance in the lives of those around Him. Nathaniel became convinced that Jesus was the Messiah after Jesus related a vision He had of Nathaniel sitting under a fig tree (John 1:48). The Samaritan woman inspired many to believe because she declared, "He told me all that I ever did" (John 4:39).

God intends us to be a people who declare the message of the Kingdom in word and deed—preaching and demonstrating the power of the message. The Church has lived far below God's intentions for far too long. When we equate our paltry experience with God's best, we believe a lie. God wills for us to have a lifestyle that aligns with His. This is the key to understanding God's desire for Church reformation in this hour. God is calling us to live up to His original design for the Church—which He promised to build, and against which the gates of hell will not prevail. The following principles offer guidance for the Church to become a supernatural community that reflects God's eternal standards. In discussing these standards we'll place particular emphasis on the life and ministry of Jesus on earth and the life and experience of the early Church.

1. We must preach the gospel in word and deed. Scripture everywhere illustrates the essential pattern of proclamation and demonstration. Jesus, our model, declared the message of the Kingdom while demonstrating the miraculous so that all would believe. Jesus told the Pharisees that if they didn't believe His words, they could at least believe in the works He performed (John 10:38). After Jesus' ascension, the Apostles continued to proclaim and demonstrate the gospel according to the divine pattern Jesus had taught them.

Our ability to bring God's supernatural intervention makes us immediately relevant to those around us. When the planners of the wedding at Cana did not provide enough wine for their guests—a major social embarrassment—Jesus turned water into wine (John 2). When Lazarus died outside of God's time, Jesus brought His friend back to life (John 11). After crossing the Sea of Galilee, Jesus provided food in abundance to those who had nothing to eat (John 6). Miracles point people to the one true God. The ministry of Paul further exemplifies the combination of preaching and demonstration:

For I will not dare to speak of any of those things which Christ has not accomplished through me, in word and deed,

to make the Gentiles obedient—in mighty signs and wonders, by the power of the Spirit of God, so that ... I have
fully preached the gospel of Christ (Romans 15:18-19).

MIRACLES POINT PEOPLE TO THE ONE TRUE GOD.

2. **A life of power is the will of God**. Our born again experience
instilled us with the divine nature of God (Colossians 1:27). God
not only wants His children to do what Jesus did, but also calls
us higher—to greater works than those performed by Jesus (John
14:12). God never intended us to be dependant on this world's
resources or to live at the mercy of every circumstance. We are to
live with God-consciousness, knowing we possess every resource
needed to pull down strongholds and cast down every high thing
that exalts itself against the knowledge of God (2 Corinthians 10:4-
5). We must set our faces like flint, refusing to be comfortable with
powerlessness in our lives.

3. **We must preach and teach with power**. The proclamation
of the good news was never intended to sound like a sales pitch. The
Kingdom proclamation summons the words of eternity that introduce people to the Person of Jesus, who is the living embodiment
of God's original and best intention for our lives. God's proclamation power can put entire cities and regions under the conviction of
the Holy Spirit so that multitudes may be swept into the Kingdom
(Acts 13:44; 2:41).

When Peter proclaimed the first message of the New Testament
Church in Acts 2:14, he used a word also found in Acts 2:4 when
the disciples began to speak in tongues as the Holy Spirit "gave them
utterance" (Wagner Commentary Book of Acts). Skillful human
rhetoric could not produce the impact of Peter's sermon—its impact

occurred only by supernatural power. In this coming season, God is going to release words that believers will carry with great force into the church and marketplace. Millions will be supernaturally compelled to accept the message of the Kingdom of God. Multitudes are waiting to respond to our message—if we would only put the message into practice according to God's divine design. Jesus said the harvest would be plentiful, but the laborers would be few in this hour (Matthew 9:37).

4. The promises of Scripture are invitations to believe and are not automatic. Scripture is replete with promises for those who call upon God's name. He intends for us to be a people who do the works of Jesus and even greater works (John 14:12). He wants us to be victorious in every area of our lives (Romans 8:37), and He intends to pour out His spirit on all flesh (Joel 2:28). But these promises require our alignment with Him. If we lack in agreement, engagement, or alignment, it will result in an abortion of God's promises for this current season. We desperately need greater encounter with God so that we can live in accordance with His timing for what He wants to accomplish.

In the closing moments of Jesus' life, the Apostle Peter abandoned Him, despite having walked closely with Jesus as a member of His inner circle for almost three-and-a-half-years. Yet through divine encounter with the Holy Spirit on the day of Pentecost, Peter was empowered to preach the first sermon of the New Testament Church wherein 3,000 souls were converted (Acts 2:4, 41). In the next chapter, Luke tells of a man who had been lame since birth. Studying the man, Peter boldly declared, "Silver and gold I do not have, but what I do have I give you: In the name of Jesus Christ of Nazareth, rise up and walk" (Acts 3:6). The lame man is healed because he met a man of great divine encounter, one who lived in accordance with heaven's promises.

One of the keys to divine encounter is alignment with God's prophetic promises. Jesus launched His public ministry by quoting Isaiah 61:1-3 in the synagogue. He was aligning Himself publically with God's divine destiny for His life. After declaring God's promise over His life, He declared that He fulfilled it, even before completing the full measure of His assignment (Luke 4:21). Prophetic destiny is fulfilled through our alignment with all God has spoken.

5. We must cultivate the fear of the Lord. As we pursue God's invitation to come into alignment with His prophetic promises, God wants to mark us with the fear of the Lord. The fear of the Lord and encounter go hand-in-hand. A healthy fear of the Lord allows us to approach God properly and to tremble at His word. There's a beauty God imparts to His children as we behold Him; there's a release of the fear of the Lord that results in our desiring nothing but Him with every fiber of our being, and where all we want is to be used for His glory.

God marked the early believers with the fear of the Lord. The early Church walked in power because of a synergistic relationship between divine encounter and the fear of the Lord. The fear of the Lord wasn't a Sunday sermon series, but a living, breathing reality birthed through deep encounter. Recognizing our need for God births the fear of the Lord. Despite emerging from a hostile environment, the early Church grew and advanced continuously. When opposition came, they called on the name of the Lord to increase the grace that was upon them, and the Father desires to do the same today.

God is unveiling a deep revelation of the fear of the Lord in the body of Christ today. I believe the prophetic teacher Paul Cain was right on target when he declared, "To the Church without mixture I will give the Spirit without measure." The deepest desire of heaven is to release the Spirit without measure on the people of God.

THE EARLY CHURCH WALKED IN POWER BECAUSE OF A
SYNERGISTIC RELATIONSHIP BETWEEN DIVINE ENCOUNTER AND
THE FEAR OF THE LORD—IT WAS A LIVING, BREATHING REALITY
BIRTHED THROUGH DEEP ENCOUNTER.

Much like Peter—a mere man imbued with so much power that those in surrounding towns were healed by his shadow—God wants to release unlimited grace and power upon the saints of God to impact the world. With such power comes great responsibility, and only a deep revelation of the fear of the Lord can help us steward this season properly.

6. We must give ourselves to discipling others. With the mandate to minister with the works of Jesus, comes a responsibility to equip others for the work of the ministry. Paul pointed to the five-fold ministry offices as the primary means of bringing this to pass. "And He Himself gave some to be apostles, some prophets, some evangelists, and some pastors and teachers, for the equipping of the saints for the work of ministry, for the edifying of the body of Christ" (Ephesians 4:11-12).

Jesus' Kingdom proclamations included demonstrations of power, but He equally committed Himself to empowering His disciples to do the same. Leaders in the body of Christ should embrace this as their pattern for today. The foundation for equipping people who demonstrate the power of God is leaders committed to living in this power themselves. What's more, this leadership commitment in the body of Christ will inspire recognition of our great need for God.

At every available opportunity, Jesus used experience to train His disciples. When calling His disciples, Jesus used a word of knowledge to meet them at their point of need. The three fishermen worked all night and had caught nothing (Luke 5:5). Jesus simply instructed them to drop their nets again (Luke 5:4), and a story of scarcity becomes one of abundance. This display of God's divine power changed Peter's world, along with James and John, and helped them recognize their great need for God (Luke 5:1-11). You know the rest of the story—they left all to follow Him. But it's important to note that the disciples weren't called to recite a prayer, but to experience life with Him. The perquisite was that they needed to forsake all to follow Him (Luke 14:33; 5:11). According the Father's grand design, they would do the same works He was doing after they learned and experienced His life through dynamic personal relationship.

His first miracle was instructive to help the disciples understand and believe that Jesus was who He said He was. He turned water into wine, and John concludes the story with this exceptional statement:

> This beginning of signs Jesus did in Cana of Galilee, and manifested His glory; and His disciples believed in Him (John 2:11).

The disciples believed in Jesus because of the miracle they witnessed. Experiencing miracles up close was a vital aspect of Jesus' discipleship training process and is no less important for discipleship today. Jesus also trained His disciples in the anatomy of miracles by performing miracles with the participation of those around Him. At the Cana wedding, He commanded unknown people to fill six vats with water and then draw it out (John 2:6-7). In the feeding of 5,000, Jesus asked for what few resources the disciples possessed (the five barley loaves and two fishes), multiplied it, and fed all who were present (Mark 6:37-44). With a word from Jesus, Peter became the first mortal man to walk on water (Matthew 15:22-33). Jesus, as His Father's representative, longed to show God's intention to partner with humanity in performing miracles. Jesus used the resources of those around Him, and they experienced miracles personally as they obeyed His heaven-sent commands. The same holds true for us today.

Jesus also released the disciples two-by-two to go out and preach the gospel with great power. Having seen countless miracles with their own eyes, the disciples were empowered by Jesus to do the same. Luke later records that Jesus similarly released seventy others to preach and heal in His name.

> After these things the Lord appointed seventy others also, and sent them two by two before His face into every city and place where He Himself was about to go. Then He said to them, "The harvest truly is great, but the laborers *are* few; therefore pray the Lord of the harvest to send out laborers into His harvest" (Luke 10:1-2).

In sending seventy others, Jesus was saying that there is an abundance of people ready to receive Him as the desire of the nations (Haggai 2:7). What was required to reach them was a group of believers willing to partner with Him in the preaching and demonstration of the Kingdom. The harvest is already assured when we come into alignment with God's standards.

A divine shift is taking place in the universal Church, where the saints of God will step on the world's stage to release His glory as never before.

God is raising up fearless leaders across the globe that will demand nothing less from themselves—and from those they train—than proclamation of the Kingdom with demonstration of God's power. Young and old will be filled with the power of heaven, never-before-seen miracles will be demonstrated through human hands, and Jesus will be magnified in the earth.

GOD IS FORMING US INTO A PROPHETIC PEOPLE. GOD HAS PROVIDED EVERY TOOL WE'LL NEED TO CHANGE THE WORLD. WE'LL BE LIMITED ONLY BY OUR FAILURE TO HEAR AND DECLARE WHAT THE FATHER IS SPEAKING.

CHAPTER SIX

PROPHETIC WORDS THAT CREATE OUR FUTURE

Summer eclipsed spring, and crisp fall weather arrived to greet day 300 of continuous worship in the city of South Bend, Indiana. The stadium gathering has moved to Joyce Center at the Notre Dame campus, where several media sources provide daily coverage of what most in the community call "God's Meeting."

As the gatherings continue and the weeks roll by, visitors number into the millions, and the power and presence of God continues to manifest with increasing intensity. The thousands who gather each evening never complain of boredom. Some come for a few hours but end up staying for days, and others who arrived last spring from across the world have never left. It's like a slice of heaven in Joyce Center—an intimate, transformative experience of worship.

This invasion of God's presence and power is far beyond what believers expected to experience in their lifetimes. Some ask if God had provided any previous indication that He would move with such power in South Bend. This was partially answered on day 140 when William Johnson ministered to 17,000 people in attendance, including John and Diana Robinson.

Johnson, a fifth-generation Assemblies of God minister, has pastored South Bend's First Assembly of God since 1983. He tells the attendees that First Assembly of God was the only church he'd ever had the privilege of pastoring and that at age twenty-one he and his wife surrendered to the call of God on their lives and traveled to churches throughout the Midwest to conduct healing and miracle crusades. He saw the power of God at work, healing the sick and delivering those who were oppressed of demons. He and his wife, Jennifer, were committed to seeing a powerful move of God in South Bend and another Great Awakening across the United States.

While life on the road had its challenges, Pastor William Johnson shared that he and his wife learned to love it. More importantly, they loved seeing hundreds of people transformed by the power of the gospel.

William and his wife were scheduled to minister at a one-week crusade at First Assembly of God in South Bend during the fall of 1983. Despite the fact that their pastor of five years had resigned to lead a congregation on the west coast, the church board decided to continue with the crusade as planned, believing it would be a source of great encouragement for the people. "As Jennifer and I pulled our R.V. into the parking lot of First Assembly of God, we heard the audible voice of the Holy Spirit say, 'Welcome to your new home.' Never having heard the audible voice of God, I was startled and asked my wife if she had heard the same thing. She had indeed heard the same voice."

Pastor William and his wife hid these words from God in their hearts. The first week of the crusade was such a powerful time in God's presence that the church board extended their stay another week. They agreed to stay. The head of the church board approached the couple after the final night of the crusade and shared a dream he had the evening before the crusade began. In this dream God revealed that William and Jennifer were to be the new pastors of the church. He asked the board to fast and pray throughout the first week of the crusade to confirm what God had revealed, which He did for each board member before they had even broached the subject with William and his wife. The couple graciously accepted the call to be pastors of First Assembly of God in South Bend. They settled in the parsonage next to the Church and had a wonderful time getting to know many of the people who are still members today. "The church welcomed us with open arms, and I did my best to serve them, even though I had very little experience," Pastor William explained.

"I hadn't attended seminary or Bible College. In fact, the only thing I had done was to say *yes* to the call of God on my life. Jennifer was pregnant with our first child, and I remember feeling very dissatisfied with my ministry efforts during the first year. I shared with the congregation all the messages I had received from God during my time of itinerant ministry, and they seemed to enjoy the messages. But I was still dissatisfied. I longed to see the power of God displayed as it was in the Gospels. The church had grown to 100 people in the first year of our pastorate, but I wasn't satisfied with that—I wanted to see a manifestation of the glory of God!

> JESUS IS CALLING THAT WHICH IS UNSEEN OR NON-EXISTENT TO COME ALIVE IN THE BODY OF CHRIST—CHURCHES AND GROUPS THAT ARE SPIRITUALLY DEAD TO COME BACK TO LIFE IN THIS HOUR.

"In desperation and in full agreement with my wife, I decided to spend three days in fasting and prayer at the church. I also invited two church board members to join me. We began the three-day fast by simply praying and worshipping in the church sanctuary and coming together every few hours to share anything God had shown us. The first day seemed to be the toughest because our bodies were acclimating to not eating, even though we drank plenty of water. Each of us identified areas of our lives where we needed to repent at the close of the first day. We confessed our sins and prayed for each other and retired for the night on cots in the small offices of the church.

"I had no premonition that the Holy Spirit would communicate a life-changing vision to me as I dozed off. It was exactly 4 a.m. on Friday, October 19, 1984. I remember glancing at a small digital clock after being startled from my sleep when something like a movie screen dropped down in front of my cot and began displaying a vision:

"I saw a dead body on stage with young people speaking life into it. And the Holy Spirit said to me, 'I will do this in the natural, but also in the spiritual.' The Holy Spirit is calling forth a generation of life from death. Yes—Jesus is the resurrection and the life, and He's calling this generation that seems so spiritually empty back to life. He's calling that which is unseen or non-existent to come alive in the body of Christ—churches and groups that are spiritually dead to come back to life in this hour. The call is clear. Those who want to be part of what He's doing must be attuned to what the Spirit is saying in this hour. I seek to revive by raising all that's dead back to life. As the townspeople took notice when Lazarus rose from the dead, so too will the nations take notice when I raise to life all that I want to revive in this place, God shared with me.

"I saw the glory of God descending on a stadium that was filled to capacity. They weren't there to meet with a man or attend a meeting. They were hungry for God. As they worshipped, healings took place. Creative healings, like ears growing where there were none before, blind eyes opening that had never seen the light of day, muscles growing back, and ligaments coming back into place. The Holy Spirit was orchestrating everything.

"The worship music was quite simple, but a cloud of the manifest presence of God hovered over the stage as everyone sang. Angels appeared and entered into worship, and there appeared to be an open heaven above the heads of those who ministered on the stage. I was reminded of Jacob's ladder in Genesis 28.

"A young man stood to speak, encouraging the people to press into everything that the Holy Spirit was doing. He also asked God for more of His fire to fall, and fireballs immediately descended from heaven and fell on the heads of the people. The power of God hit them like an electrical current, and many fell out, weeping and shaking under the power of God.

"A deep sense of brokenness pervaded and all were completely in awe of what the Holy Spirit was doing throughout the stadium. Reporters told of the thousands who came to meet with God. Some tried to criticize the move of God but were immediately convicted by their actions, while others received calls from their home to ask about reported appearances of fire above the stadium. Local bars emptied out, and people flocked to the stadium in droves to find out what was going on. A body was brought into the stadium, and the crowd united to declare, 'Live! Live!' Others held their Bibles in the air and cried out for Jesus to be glorified through the resurrection of this person.

"Now the scene moved outside the stadium to the flow of traffic from the city heading toward the massive stadium. The billboard outside declared 'God is in the house, 21st day: Come any time to meet with God.' The lights were on in the stadium, and another young man was preaching. He appeared to be Hispanic. In fact, he preached in Spanish, and it was being translated into English. He simply declared the work of Jesus on the cross. He called forward those who need Jesus in their life. Many came, including many Hispanics. Half of those who responded to the call of salvation were now on their backs, and some were slithering around on the ground as if demon possessed. The young man declared that where sin abounds the grace of God abounds much more. People ran to those who were demon possessed and declared that the demons must leave in the name of Jesus.

"The scene then switched back to the crowd standing and simply worshipping. The presence of the Holy Spirit was evident. A young man introduced the mayor of the city, although I couldn't identify the city or nation in which this was taking place. The mayor stood up and declared the city to be a refuge and a sanctuary for the Most High God. He also stated that he's been on the phone with other mayors from around the country who also want to publically declare their cities to be sanctuaries for the Most High God, Jesus Christ. This is how the vision ended."

As Pastor William shares the prophetic vision he received twenty-eight years ago, the presence of God fills the arena. Those in attendance can't help but see the strong parallels between the vision and this current move of God. Concurrently hundreds, if not thousands begin to have their own prophetic encounters right there. It's as though the Spirit of truth is bearing witness to Himself. As the vision is shared, the door is opened for those listening to have a similar experience.

Pastor William continues to speak, "I really didn't know how to handle the vision that God gave me. I thought perhaps this amazing move would begin as I addressed my congregation the following Sunday. But I knew deep in my heart that the vision was much larger than my church and that a kairos moment in history would be needed for the vision to take place. My wife and I have had offers to lucrative ministry positions, but each time I recalled this vision of the Holy Spirit.

"This is only the third time I've shared this vision in public. The first time was with my congregation the second Sunday after I received it. The second time was a few years later at a regional gathering of Assemblies of God ministers where I taught on spiritual renewal. The leaders and I felt it would be appropriate to share it again tonight because, as many of you know, we made a commitment to pray, seek the direction of God, and respond to what we believe He's speaking. Our right response to the word of the Lord will enable us to receive the full measure of the Father's outpouring in the earth for this season."

The leaders also feel a strong leading to see God-ordained government put into place, where those called to fill the office of Apostle are publically recognized to serve as senior leaders in this citywide move of God. The leaders are already functioning in this capacity, but there will be a time of public recognition very soon (Ephesians 4:11). The leaders also believe this move in the city of South Bend isn't some fleeting or evanescent phenomenon but part of a larger reformation that's ordained of God to bring healing to the nations.

Pastor William asks Heather Brown to join him on the platform. He explains that Heather is a prophetess who has encouraged the congregation at First Assembly for many years. "The leadership team and I believe she has a key prophetic word to share with us in this season of reformation and revival in South Bend," he says, as Heather Brown approaches the stage and begins to prophesy:

> The Spirit of reformation has been released into the earth. God says, "I am about to change the face of Christianity within a generation so that it has the same Spirit of boldness and tenacity as Martin Luther. In this next reformation, I'll pour out My Spirit on a people who are desperate and longing for Me, who desire nothing less than to see Me glorified in the earth.
>
> "Old Church structures, forms, and modes will come down to make way for the emerging wineskin with which I'll clothe My people in this hour. The Spirit of wisdom and revelation will be poured out on the earth so My people can enjoy the fullness of what I created them to be. Those who have ears to hear and eyes to see will access realms of My Spirit previously thought to be impossible.
>
> "Yes, this new Spirit of reformation declares: 'With God nothing is impossible.' Yes, the portals of heaven are open so

nothing shall be impossible for My people in this hour. Continue to pursue Me, and you will become fascinated with knowing Me. What my people behold in this hour—that is what they will become. As they overcome seeming impossibilities in My name, they will see My eternal purposes come to pass. As they behold unsaved loved ones returning to Me, so it shall be. As they see entire nations come to Me, so shall it be, and My Kingdom will come to earth as never before.

"What they see in the Spirit, they will manifest in the earth so that My Kingdom can be established in the earth. Realize that you are living in an unprecedented hour when the Spirit has come to reveal Me to the nations. Are you frustrated? Are burned out? Are you longing for more of Me? Yes, I have placed My people in desperate and tough situations so that they turn to Me in this hour!

"Many have realized that what they desire can never come to pass without a visitation from the God of the impossible. Listen to the voice of My Spirit tonight and receive what you desire. You too will receive the reward of your travail on behalf of My Kingdom. For this is the hour of change, and all who embrace it will be part of the new reformation. Yes, no man can conceive what I am doing, and no man will receive glory for what I am about to do. For this hour of visitation is My hour—this is the hour when all things become new!"

HEARING AND WALKING IN OUR INHERITANCE

An Old Testament prophecy with great relevance to our lives under the new covenant is Joel 2:28 where the prophet declares that God will pour out His "spirit on all flesh." In describing what will take place, Joel declares that sons and daughters will prophesy, old men will dream dreams, and young men will see visions. This is a picture of the future when God pours His Spirit on everyone.

During the time when the Old Testament was written, prophets alone were privileged to speak for God and make declarations about the future. But the pouring out of the Holy Spirit on the day of Pentecost inaugurated a dramatic shift. The prophetic Spirit, which had come upon a chosen few, now could be had by "all who would call upon the name of the Lord." The Apostle Peter, the first senior leader of the New Testament church, declared on the day of Pentecost, "But this is what was spoken by the prophet Joel" (Acts 2:16).

The Father has given the Church the gift of prophecy to build the future that God intends for His Church and to declare His purposes and intentions in any given situation—equally applicable to individuals, organizations, regions, cities, and nations of the world.

The Church will enter uncharted territory during this season of reformation, a spiritual dimension beyond anything we've seen before. One essential tool the Father has provided to help us during this time is the gift of prophecy. In Joel's prophecy, God expressed His intention to pour out His Spirit on all flesh, similar to the way wine is poured into a wineskin: "And no one puts new wine into old wineskins; or else the new wine bursts the wineskins, the wine is spilled, and the wineskins are ruined. But new wine must be put into new wineskins" (Mark 2:22).

This new wine represents a continuous and fresh Holy Spirit outpouring—that which God promised to pour on all flesh. The Church can be likened to the wineskin, but we'll never possess the life, vitality and fruit which God desires until we're filled with the new wine. The Church must be renewed before it can carry the new wine. And God *will* renew wineskin, making it flexible and pliable as it responds and obeys the voice of the Creator. God's desire is to govern His Church the same way He governs individuals: by His voice. Scripture illustrates that the Father's emphasis may change from season to season. Prophetic ministry is in the DNA of the New Testament Church and will be central to all God wants to achieve in this coming hour.

> IT IS GOD'S DESIRE TO GOVERN HIS CHURCH THE SAME WAY HE GOVERNS INDIVIDUALS: BY HIS VOICE. PROPHETIC MINISTRY IS IN THE DNA OF NEW TESTAMENT CHURCH AND WILL BE CENTRAL TO ALL GOD WANTS TO ACHIEVE IN THIS COMING HOUR.

Prophecy is essential to the community of believers. Prophecy reveals the higher purpose of stewarding the earth, which we were designed to fulfill, stirring our imaginations and inspiring us to come up higher and go above and beyond all we dreamed possible. Conversely, "Where there is no prophetic vision the people cast off restraint, but blessed is he who keeps the law" (Proverbs 29:18, ESV).

Nearly every prophet in the Old Testament spoke about this present hour of messianic fulfillment. We have already fulfilled prophecy by becoming sons and daughters of God. We partake of the same grace as God's prophetic spokespersons in the Old Testament thousands of years ago. We are the sons of the prophets with thousands of years of prophetic history as our inheritance (Acts 3:25).

A PROPHETIC PEOPLE

Prophetic ministry is essential to the New Testament Church, foundational to the way God plans to shape the earth. When God's heart is revealed through prophecy, we get a picture of what God intends for the future. Prophecy can change reality as we know it and help us overcome every seeming impossibility that opposes the will of God for our lives. The people of God have yet to experience the essence of prophecy—the power of the declared word—in all of its fullness. Prophetic declaration has the power to change the world.

We find God speaking the universe into existence in Genesis 1:3, "Then God said, 'Let there be light;' and there was light." Of particular interest is the way it was created: by the Father, Son, and Holy Spirit collaborating. This is a clear indication of God's powerful spoken word and the eternal significance behind His ordained prophetic utterances.

Genesis 1:3

Then He said, "Let there be light," and there was light.

Genesis 1:11

Then He said, "Let the earth bring forth grass, the herb that yields seed, and the fruit tree that yields fruit according to its kind, whose seed is in itself, on the earth," and it was so.

Genesis 1:14

Then He said, "Let there be lights in the firmament of the heavens to divide the day from the night; and let them be for signs and seasons, and for days and years.

Genesis 1:20

Then He said, "Let the waters abound with an abundance of

living creatures, and let birds fly above the earth across the face of the firmament of the heavens."

Genesis 1:24

Then He said, "Let the earth bring forth the living creature according to its kind: cattle and creeping thing and beast of the earth, *each* according to its kind," and it was so.

Genesis 1:26

Then He said, "Let Us make man in Our image, according to Our likeness; let them have dominion over the fish of the sea, over the birds of the air, and over the cattle, over all the earth and over every creeping thing that creeps on the earth."

God's plan for earth was executed when God spoke what He wanted into existence. He created Adam as the perfect man, imbued with God's thoughts, purposes, and intentions. At God's commission Adam named every animal in existence. God spoke the universe into existence, but He empowered man to build it according to His plan, calling forth the names of the animals. Equally, God has commissioned the saints to co-labor with God, using the prophetic word to shape the earth according to His eternal plan. Words carry negative or positive power and will determine the history of the world (Proverbs 18:21). The people of God must see, hear, and declare accordingly for the earth to come into the fullness the Father

---

GOD HAS COMMISSIONED THE SAINTS TO CO-LABOR WITH GOD, USING THE PROPHETIC WORD TO SHAPE THE EARTH ACCORDING TO HIS ETERNAL PLAN. THE PEOPLE OF GOD MUST SEE, HEAR, AND DECLARE ACCORDINGLY FOR THE EARTH TO COME INTO THE FULLNESS THE FATHER INTENDS.

---

intends. The gift of prophecy flows out of friendship with God. He delights to give this knowledge of the future to His beloved children, as Jesus affirmed when describing the role of the Holy Spirit in the believer's life in John 16:13:

> However, when He, the Spirit of truth, has come, He will guide you into all truth; for He will not speak on His own authority, but whatever He hears He will speak; and He will tell you things to come.

As friends and co-laborers with God, we get to help the Father bring the future—the prophetic fulfillment of His plan—into the here and now. As God speaks, He desires that His children be in alignment with His purposes, so they, too, can speak as He does. When we speak, our words must be invested with His divine authority and purpose.

God declared His intention to build a nation through Abraham when his wife was far beyond her childbearing years. Abraham believed God and gave Him glory for what He had spoken. He made a declaration of faith and sealed it through his praise to God. Abraham's praise became a prophecy of what God intended in the earth. Paul writes about Abraham,

> As it is written, "I have made you a father of many nations" … He became the father of many nations, according to what was spoken, "So shall your descendants be." And not being weak in faith, he did not consider his own body, already dead (since he was about a hundred years old), and the deadness of Sarah's womb. He did not waver at the promise of God through unbelief, but was strengthened in faith, giving glory to God, and being fully convinced that what He had promised He was also able to perform (Romans 4:17-21.

A literal translation could read, "God calls into being what does not exist as (easily as He calls) that which does exist."[10] The power to create begins in heaven as God reveals His plans to His friends on earth. These friends align with His plans by declaring them on earth. "As you believe, so you should speak," the Apostle Paul admonished the Church in Corinth:

> And since we have the same spirit of faith, according to what is written, "I believed and therefore I spoke," we also believe and therefore speak (2 Corinthians 4:13).

Other than Adam in the Garden of Eden, Enoch was the first man described as having walked with God. The phrase "walking with God" can be defined as constant and familiar relationship. Scripture reveals two remarkable things about the man who walked in constant discourse with God: Enoch prophesied about the future and was translated to heaven by faith, never experiencing death (Genesis 5:24, Hebrews 11:5, Jude 1:14). I believe Enoch represents a type of believer that God is raising up in this day: a friend of God who prophesies and enters into the future by faith.

THE LORD WANTS US TO INHERIT A PROPHETIC GRACE THAT THE CHURCH HAS NEVER EXPERIENCED. PROPHETIC GRACE CAN BE DEFINED AS THE GIFT BIRTHED FROM FRIENDSHIP TO SEE, HEAR, AND DECLARE THE FATHER'S INTENTION THAT SHAPES THE HISTORY OF THE WORLD.

The Lord wants us to inherit a prophetic grace that the Church has never experienced. Prophetic grace can be defined as the gift birthed from friendship to see, hear, and declare the Father's

---

[10] Pfeiffer, C. F., and Harrison, E. F. (1962). *The Wycliffe Bible Commentary: New Testament* (Ro 4:17). Chicago: Moody Press.

intention that shapes the history of the world. The Apostle Paul says of this coming glory,

> But if the ministry of death, written and engraved on stones, was glorious, so that the children of Israel could not look steadily at the face of Moses because of the glory of his countenance ... how will the ministry of the Spirit not be more glorious? For if the ministry of condemnation had glory, the ministry of righteousness exceeds much more in glory.... For if what is passing away was glorious, what remains is much more glorious (2 Corinthians 3:7-11).

Paul references the glory emanating from the face of Moses. Moses had such a deep encounter with God that his face emitted blinding light—the children of Israel couldn't even look at him. But as glorious as this was, the coming glory God designed for us to experience under the new covenant will far exceed anything that took place under the old covenant.

Contextually, the glory available to us is not *limited* to prophetic grace, but certainly *includes* prophetic grace. The glory of God came upon many of His spokespersons in the Old Testament: Moses, who performed signs and wonders before an entire nation (Deuteronomy 34:10-12), Elisha the prophet, who revealed the secret stratagems of the king of Syria, an enemy of God's people (2 Kings 6:8-12), and Daniel the prophet, who interpreted the dreams of King Nebuchadnezzar (Daniel 4:1-9). These prophets used the glory that came upon them to shape the destinies of nations. But we've been given our own prophetic promise in this hour: "For if what is passing away was glorious, what remains is much more glorious" (2 Corinthians 3:11).

God is looking for faithful stewards in this wonderful moment in history! The Apostle Paul admonishes, "Let a man so consider us, as servants of Christ and stewards of the mysteries of God. Moreover it is required in stewards that one be found faithful" (1 Corinthians 4:1-2).

We will be considered faithful stewards as we obey what God has spoken. James describes deception as hearing but not responding to God's commands (James 1:22). What's more, we should declare His word and celebrate His intervention in our lives continuously. In teaching the nation of Israel how they were to love Him with all their heart, soul, and strength (Deuteronomy 6:4-9), God commanded that they continually declare His word and remember His intervention in their lives:

> And these words which I command you today shall be in your heart. You shall teach them diligently to your children, and shall talk of them when you sit in your house, when you walk by the way, when you lie down, and when you rise up. You shall bind them as a sign on your hand, and they shall be as frontlets between your eyes. You shall write them on the doorposts of your house and on your gates (Deuteronomy 6:6-9).

God wanted His chosen people, Israel, to declare the future He had planned for them. Tragically, they chose to reject His promises and focus on their obstacles. They failed to appropriate the promises of God even though they were clearly instructed to do so. We face the similar, sobering possibility when we fail to align ourselves with what God is speaking in this hour (Numbers 14:23).

We become doers of the word as we seek to obey the word of God and give it preeminence in our lives. Jesus taught that we must pay close attention to what God has spoken and that we will be positioned for increase when we do so.

THE FUTURE WILL BELONG TO THOSE WHO SEE AND DECLARE
WHAT GOD INTENDS FOR THE EARTH.

Therefore take heed how you hear. For whoever has, to him more will be given; and whoever does not have, even what he seems to have will be taken from him (Luke 8:18).

The Father's desire has not yet been fully manifested in the earth (Matthew 6:10). Jesus had a desire to "share many things" with the disciples but was unable to do so because they were not ready to receive them (John 16:12). But He said that the Person of the Holy Spirit would guide them into all truth. In His wisdom and mercy, the Holy Spirit doesn't reveal all we need to know at one moment of time. He unveils Himself over time through the process of intimacy and encounter. We become candidates for deeper revelation as we demonstrate our fidelity and careful obedience to what has already been entrusted to us.

But he who received seed on the good ground is he who hears the word and understands it, who indeed bears fruit and produces: some a hundredfold, some sixty, some thirty (Matthew 13:23).

God wants to reveal His will and purposes to His children so they can declare them and fulfill His prophetic intention to restore the earth to its proper order.

I have put My words in your mouth; I have covered you with the shadow of My hand, that I may plant the heavens, lay the foundations of the earth, and say to Zion, "You are My people" (Isaiah 51:16).

The future will belong to those who see and declare what God intends for the earth. The Father's goal is not a prophetic movement. He is interested in making us into a prophetic people. He wants His people to *be* signs and wonders, not simply to perform them. Samuel the prophet serves as a great figure to study in order to see what characteristics God looks for in His prophetic people.

1. Samuel was consecrated to God as a Nazarite before he was born. Nazarites were separated and consecrated for service to God. The Lord requires the same of His believers today. The Holy Spirit longs for an undivided heart. The fear of the Lord will be released to burn in our hearts as we pursue God with singleness of purpose. There is a correlation between the continuous flow of the Spirit and the fear of the Lord. The more we fear Him, the greater measure of the prophetic Spirit we will receive.

2. Samuel grew in favor with God and man (1 Samuel 2:26). The Son of God grew in favor with God and man (Luke 2:52). We too must grow in favor with God, but we must not neglect growing in favor with man if we are to fulfill God's plan for the earth. Having favor with man is greater than finances, position, or influence because it opens the door to the impossible. God is going to release the people of God into positions of unprecedented favor and strategic influence in society as we demonstrate our faithful stewardship of all that He has spoken.

3. God used Samuel's intercession to bring victory. After several defeats, God used the intercession and the sacrifices of Samuel to defeat the archenemy of Israel, the Philistines. Prophetic people understand their role and responsibility to stand between God and man, interceding for the will of God to be established. This reminds me of an experience I had a number of years ago while ministering in Brazil. The morning service was charged with the awesome presence of God. We were slated to meet again that evening, where God had directed us to minister through the laying of hands. As the morning service concluded the pastor mentioned that I would be giving each person a prophetic word during the ministry time. While I had not planned to minister in that manner, I ministered prophetically to each person as I had been asked. I recall ministering to a few young ladies, and God had His hand on their lives—I could sense that they had a tremendous purpose and destiny. I was impressed that they wrote down everything I said to them, and it caused me to understand the idea of standing between God and man—declaring His word and works—in a marvelous new way.

4. Samuel operated in multiple spheres of influence (1 Samuel 7). Israel recognized Samuel not only as prophet but also as judge. As a judge, he functioned with full military, judicial, and priestly authority. Similarly, the saints of God will serve in multiple spheres of influence in the coming movement of the Spirit that God will pour out on His people. The saints of God will be imbued with unprecedented favor to influence and shape our culture through prophetic declarations that will touch every sphere of society.

5. Samuel calls two kings into their assignments (1 Samuel 12 and 1 Samuel 16). Prophets and those with the prophetic Spirit will be given access to the highest places of authority in every nation. Nations will stand strong or fall according to their response to the word of the Lord. Prophets will call men and women to rise up and fulfill their God-given destinies.

6. Power rested on Samuel's words. God did not allow one word of the prophets to fall to the ground (1 Samuel 3:19). The words of Samuel were never wasted but carried with them the grace and power to change the landscape of a nation. Samuel spoke as the friend and spokesperson of God in the earth. God is releasing a revelation of the power of words and how prophetic words have the power to change individuals, cities, and nations. The lips of the righteous feed many (Proverbs 10:21).

God is forming us into a prophetic people, and He has provided every tool we'll need to change the world. We'll be limited only by our failure to hear and declare what the Father is speaking. The words the Father speaks are Spirit and life and have unlimited potential (John 6:63). As a prophetic people, God is inviting us to walk a path that has never been trod so that generations coming after us may inherit a better planet. God will anchor heaven here on earth as we release His eternal word.

God is forming us into a prophetic people. God has provided every tool we'll need to change the world. We'll be limited only by our failure to hear and declare what the Father is speaking.

OUR IDENTITY STEMS FROM AN ONGOING UNDERSTANDING OF WHAT'S ALREADY BEEN GRANTED TO US. WE ARE A ROYAL PRIESTHOOD WHO HAVE COMPLETE FAVOR WITH OUR FATHER IN HEAVEN.

CHAPTER SEVEN

WALKING IN DESTINY: A LIFETIME PROCESS

It's 5:30 a.m., and John is the first to wake in the Robinson household. He's had little respite and even less sleep lately as he eagerly anticipates the opening of his new business, Robinson Gourmet Burgers. Today is the grand opening, and John begins it in his usual way, setting aside time for quiet contemplation and worship with the Father. As he raises his hands in worship he is overcome by feelings of gratitude at the faithfulness of God. John weeps as he recalls the countless times he and his family have witnessed the goodness of God.

As the evening sets in John recalls the first time he attended a gathering at Notre Dame stadium more than seven years ago. He faintly recalls wending his way through the stadium to find his seat, but he'll never forget what happened soon after— he was immediately transported into the first of what would be many encounters in the

Spirit. This first encounter was significant. It was where the Lord first revealed that he was to pursue his lifelong dream of owning and operating a chain of hamburger restaurants. John remembers the encounter vividly, just as he recalls the many obstacles that stood in the way. He remembers the clarity of God's voice at the time, how it helped him and his wife to keep going and never give up.

At the time of this initial encounter, John had no previous experience with owning a business, much less with starting one from scratch. He had a word from heaven but no idea where to begin, other than to begin seeking the Lord for direction at the start of each day. God seemed strangely silent on the matter, at least initially. About six months later, frustrated by the seeming silence, John cried out, "God, I believe You've spoken to me about owning a chain of restaurants, and I really need Your help. I've asked You to speak to me and show me the next step, but You remain silent."

God's reply was quick and straightforward, "John, you've heard correctly from Me, and I am working on the deep things in your heart right now because I want you to make fascination with Me the foundation of your life. As you seek Me with all your heart, I'll teach you all that you need to know concerning the dream I've given you."

John learned that he was on the right track—the voice of God was clear about that. But he also learned his most important objective was to find his fulfillment in God, not in the fulfilling of his dream.

A few months later, as God promised, John received direction about next steps. He saw a picture of himself entering through a door labeled destiny. It was uncomfortable for John to move through the door because his body felt like it was being stretched in every direction. Jesus was holding his hand, standing right beside him. As John stood observing this scene, the Holy Spirit spoke, "John, I'm working deep in your heart during this season, but I want to impart some understanding to your mind as well. I know that you never enjoyed school, but I want you to return to the University of Notre Dame and achieve your Masters of Business Administration degree. Don't be afraid. I'll provide for the cost every step of the way."

John was absolutely stunned, but the picture God revealed proved to be right on target for John. He never enjoyed high school or college, despite the fact that he was an above-average student. He wasn't thrilled at the prospect of attending an MBA program. It wasn't something he planned to do even after receiving the vision of starting his own business.

Nevertheless, John obeyed the Lord promptly and applied to the prestigious MBA program at Notre Dame University. He was accepted immediately, and God provided for tuition miraculously from two different sources throughout the two year program. The first source appeared only a few days before John was to begin classes. John and Diana received an anonymous check in the mail for the exact amount of tuition for the first year. A very wealthy businessman from John's church agreed to pay for John's second year tuition after hearing John's testimony and purpose for enrolling in the MBA program. Since the outpouring of the Holy Spirit, many churches hold to the teaching that marketplace ministry was just as important as full-time ministerial vocation.

John enjoyed the two-year program, much to his surprise, but the curriculum and workload were demanding. John continued his full-time work as a plant manager while attending classes two nights a week for three hours at a time. He continued to be active on the ministry team and also maintained his responsibilities to lead his family. At times the course work was overwhelming. John felt like quitting many times, especially when he was functioning on very little sleep. During these times, John would feel the refreshing presence of God come on him, tangibly reminding him that he was equal to the task. Since that time, John and Diana have come to embrace the vital role of obstacles in their spiritual formation.

John formed a significant relationship during his MBA studies that directly impacted his destiny. Charles Sanchez was a fellow student in the program who had recently been radically saved during the South Bend outpouring. John and Charles became fast friends, and Charles asked John to meet and mentor him in the things of God once a week. They formed a tight bond, and their families became very close.

About three years into their friendship, Charles revealed that his father was the president of the largest bank in South Bend. He took the initiative to set up a meeting with the bank's loan officer later that week so John could present his business plan. The loan officer didn't mince words, informing John that his loan proposal would have been promptly rejected were it not for his connection with the bank president. The loan officer cited John's lack of business experience and the likelihood of the venture's failure, even with a more seasoned candidate. But the bank president's personal intervention secured the matter. John received the full amount requested. This was a bona fide miracle. Three other banks had already rejected John, saying anyone willing to loan him the money would have to be out of their mind.

As John and Diana have followed God's call during the last seven years, they've encountered obstacles they could have never seen coming. Particularly painful were the challenges received at the hands of Diana's parents, who expressed grave doubts about what God was doing in their lives. Though followers of Jesus, Diana's parents criticized the move of God in South Bend, calling it "completely demonic." They also expressed concerns about the time and resources the couple was dedicating to the move of God instead of spending more time with their family. John and Diana never dreamed of Diana's parents taking such a position, but they learned to love and forgive, extending the tender grace of God instead of giving in to anger.

Diana no longer works as a schoolteacher. A young man began to writhe on the ground and shake violently, manifesting demons at the close of the school day about three years ago. Diana and another believer stepped in to help, gently holding the young man down and casting the demons out until he was completely free. But the child's parents objected to the teachers' handling of the situation and complained bitterly to the school board. After a three-month investigation, the teachers were found to have violated the school district's policy by conducting a religious exercise on school property without parental consent or assistance from a school guidance counselor. Despite the fact that the student was in much better health, Diana and her colleague were relieved of their duties. Teaching—the realization of a lifelong career goal for Diana—had been taken away in a moment simply because she tried to help a student.

God demonstrated His faithfulness to Diana three months later. John received an unexpected promotion and increase in salary at the plant, and Diana now has the opportunity to focus on raising her three children in a way she always dreamed of doing. She home schools two of her boys, John and David, and has grown tremendously in the development of her prophetic gifting. She also started painting as she is led by the Holy Spirit, and some of her beautiful prophetic creations are in high demand by family and friends. A local studio recently showcased her work, and Diana is now considering opening her own studio in the near future.

The Holy Spirit accomplished a deep work in John and Diana's hearts. Living in reliance on the Spirit has taught them to live proactively, according to God's design, rather than reactively to the world around them. They have grown immensely and overcome many obstacles, living in daily dependence and vital relationship with the Father. They have seen the faithfulness and grace of God in their lives, covering shortcomings and weaknesses. Obedience to God, to the best of their ability, has become a settled issue for the couple, and they wouldn't trade the choices they've made for anything in the world. Like many others touched by the outpouring of the Holy Spirit, the couple has learned that God wants to "do life" with His people so that His beauty can be displayed and His light can shine through them in ever-increasing measure.

THE GOD PROCESS

As I've endeavored to share throughout this book, I believe we are going to see a divine shift take place across the earth, as cities, regions, and nations align with the purposes of God. Similar to the day of Pentecost—the day the Church was birthed—we will see unique events that will reshape the world.

The Church will be released into a new spiritual dimension, and we can accelerate this process by living in vital relationship with God, where every difficulty is an opportunity to live in deeper dependence on His overcoming power. The gospel of the Kingdom was meant to address every need known to man and will flourish most prominently as chaos abounds in the earth. This is the reason He called man to have authority and to subdue an earth that, prior to the speaking of His word, was originally chaotic—void and without form (Genesis 1:1-2, 28). Although we live in a dark world, we

WE ARE GOING TO SEE A DIVINE SHIFT TAKE PLACE ACROSS THE EARTH, AS CITIES, REGIONS, AND NATIONS ALIGN WITH THE PURPOSES OF GOD. SIMILAR TO THE DAY OF PENTECOST—THE DAY THE CHURCH WAS BIRTHED—WE WILL SEE UNIQUE EVENTS THAT WILL RESHAPE THE WORLD.

have reason to rejoice. Our challenges have become a clarion call for us to rise up and introduce God's order and heavenly perspective (2 Corinthians 5:20).

Only relationship with the Father can birth the alignment God desires—through a series of ongoing encounters rather than a single spectacular event. King David defeated Goliath—a single event that became a tipping point in Israel's history. But David had a series of ongoing encounters, a history with God. He defeated a lion and then a bear (1 Samuel 17) long before he stepped into the valley with Goliath.

Throughout Scripture we discover many who modeled Christ-likeness—who functioned as *types of Christ*. Joseph, the beloved son of Jacob, was one such figure. God offers many lessons through the life of Joseph, including how God can use testings to not only shape our own destiny but that of our families and nations. Let's observe the lessons and tests that Joseph successfully navigated.

THE LESSONS OF JOSEPH

His father's favor caused jealousy and conflict. Jacob loved and favored Joseph more than his other brothers and gave his son a unique and beautiful tunic. As children of God and the Church universal, we have favor with the most important Person in the universe. It would be impossible to receive favor from a better source than the Creator of heaven and earth. Our favor with the Father aligns us to receive blessings that others will not receive—but it can also inspire jealousy in others, as seen in the life of Joseph.

God has favored us so we can steward the planet. It seems counter-intuitive, but jealousy and conflict can actually indicate the favor of God on our lives. Jesus is again our model—He faced opposition precisely because of the favor His Father placed on His life. God wants us to understand how to use His favor to overcome any opposition to our destinies (Genesis 37:3-4, Matthew 3:17, Luke 4:1-13).

Joseph's prophetic dream gave him a hope to persevere. At seventeen Joseph had a dream that was in no way connected to his present experiences and reality. It gives the Father great joy to release a vision of our future lives. Note that one piece of information left out of Joseph's dream was the opposition he'd experience during the next seventeen years. But the dream successfully anchored Joseph in hope, even in the face of betrayal by his own family. This kind of prophetic understanding of the future allows us to embrace difficulties as necessary parts of the journey. Prophetic promises instill hope for what is on the horizon. Leaning on the Father through opposition is vital to our spiritual development and positions us to handle the blessings God intends for our lives (Genesis 37:5-11, John 16:33).

Joseph's obedience to his father led to slavery. As his father had requested, Joseph visited his brothers to check on their welfare. But his brothers conspired to sell him into forced bondage with the Ishmaelites. We too will find ourselves facing adversity when we obey God. This is not without purpose. Through these testings, we can develop and become better equipped to achieve our destiny (Genesis 37:14-37).

God is not unaware of our circumstances. Joseph was betrayed by those he trusted most and thrust into circumstances he never planned for his life. But God used these divinely orchestrated unplanned events to bring Joseph into his destiny. Often the road traveled is anything but linear when an individual or community seeks to live in the fulfillment of God's prophetic word. The way things play out doesn't usually match what we planned in our heads. Jacob mourned for Joseph, thinking he had surely died, but his son was very much alive and moving closer to his destiny with each passing day according to God's grand design (Genesis 37:35-36). Joseph was being supernaturally equipped for the fulfillment of his dream even as he experienced slavery.

THE TESTINGS OF JOSEPH

It's enlightening to explore the tests and trials Joseph faced along the way, remembering that we too will face similar tests as we seek to become the reformers God destined us to be.

1. God uses the prophetic word to refine us. As prophetic teacher Graham Cooke observed, "God lives in the present-future tense." Consequently, we can see and hear what's on the horizon before it comes to pass. We are a people who live in the divine tension of present reality and promises yet to be fulfilled—a tension engineered by God that makes us rely on Him. God will allow the word of the Lord to test and refine us as He did in the life of Joseph. God ordains these times of testing until we learn to root our understanding more in His prophetic future than in our present difficulties. This anchoring in hope during times of testing builds the spiritual character we need to steward His blessings when the promises are fulfilled. The Holy Spirit leads us into the wilderness not to destroy us but to teach us how to become an oasis.

2. God watches to see how we handle our responsibilities. Long before he was Egypt's second in command, Joseph faithfully discharged the duties assigned to him on a very difficult journey. Even as a slave, Joseph knew the favor of God and prospered in all that he put his hand to (Genesis 39:1-2). His master, Potiphar, even placed him in charge of his entire household (Genesis 39:6-10). Joseph was secure in his identity and calling. True prosperity can only be achieved with a proper understanding of our position and inheritance before God. Jesus declared that the Kingdom is within us (Luke 17:21). Our identity stems from an ongoing understanding of what's already been granted to us. We are a royal priesthood who have complete favor with our Father in heaven. We may serve others, but our status as servants should not eclipse the understanding we have of our position before God.

Joseph never forgot his position before God, even as he served gladly in his master's house and as a prisoner interpreting the butler's and baker's dreams. Joseph's mindset was that of a servant and son of God, and never a victim of circumstance. We also will be assigned various levels of stewardship as we navigate through life as friends of God. We should understand our position before God so we can exercise the proper stewardship of our responsibilities. This revelation must influence everything we undertake every moment of our life.

3. God allows the enemy to test our integrity. Potiphar's wife challenged Joseph's integrity not just once, but through ongoing forceful seductions. But Joseph responded faithfully time and again based on the choices he made to serve God. He exercised free will in doing so, according to God's divine design, not as a robot. Even in the Garden of Eden, where humanity received assignment to steward the earth, God allowed satan to tempt Adam and Eve. Jesus was also challenged by satan even after the Holy Spirit led Him into the wilderness for forty days of fasting.

OUR IDENTITY STEMS FROM AN ONGOING UNDERSTANDING OF WHAT'S ALREADY BEEN GRANTED TO US. WE ARE A ROYAL PRIESTHOOD WHO HAVE COMPLETE FAVOR WITH OUR FATHER IN HEAVEN.

The great news is that God has provided the means to defeat the enemy whenever we're challenged. The Accuser will challenge God's wonderful purpose for our lives—he will try to confuse and darken our thought processes. But as we learn to think with God's mind, we "cast down arguments, and every high thing that exalts itself against the knowledge of God" (2 Corinthians 10:5). We must *choose* to think God's thoughts when hell challenges us with an alternative. Joseph's choice to follow God's path of integrity resulted in accusations of rape from Potiphar's wife, a direct consequence of his obedience to God. We must maintain our integrity regardless of the consequences. Despite the consequence of imprisonment for many years, God was nevertheless moving Joseph closer to his destiny.

4. God uses our offenses and successes to test us. Through every twist and turn, Joseph never grew bitter or angry at his circumstances. The testings in the life of Joseph are instructive to all of us as people of God. All too often, sons and daughters fall away from their God as they encounter rough waters and difficult situations. This defeatism can be provoked by the death of a close relative, a divorce, a parishioner unfairly treated by church leadership, or church leaders who have been mistreated by their flock. Regardless, we must refuse to blame the Lord for the tragedies that surround our lives. Our incomplete understanding of pain and suffering can never be an excuse for holding an offense toward God.

Twenty-two long years lapsed between the onset of Joseph's dream and its fulfillment. Finally, he ascended to great power as Egypt's second in command. What's more, Joseph did not experience justice or reconciliation with his brothers for seven more years. After twenty years, Joseph's brothers did indeed bow before him, as the dream depicted, but without knowing the Egyptian leader before them was their brother.

Joseph found himself at a crossroads. He could use his position of influence to exact revenge against his brothers, who acted wickedly, or forgive them and reconcile. At first he hid his identity, indicating perhaps that it was a decision Joseph had to wrestle with and process for a time. Joseph made the right decision, releasing grace and forgiveness to his brothers and choosing not to abuse the power of the position God had given him (Genesis 42-47).

When his time came—the fulfillment of promise—it only took a moment for Joseph to be raised from prisoner to second in command of the most powerful nation in the world. Joseph changed the destiny of nations by using his prophetic gifts and became successful beyond his wildest dreams. But even after reaching the pinnacle, he continued to discharge his duties with honor and integrity. I believe Joseph's spiritual development through testing and hardship is what enabled him to be trusted by God with exaltation. God is building the same foundation in reformers across the nations today so they can be trusted to steward the changes He has planned for the earth. The destiny of nations hangs in the balance. The greatest hour in history will come to a people who are willing to move in obedience to God's commands.

Are you ready? Will you give your full-hearted commitment to what God is doing in this hour?

AUTHOR INFORMATION

AND RESOURCES

If this book has been a blessing and help to you, please consider helping us spread the message in the following ways:

- Share the book with your family and friends
- Order additional copies for your church or ministry via www.abnersuarez.com
- Write a positive review on Amazon.com
- Post positive comments on your social media sites (i.e. Facebook, Twitter, Instagram, etc.)

We would like to stay connected with you:

- Follow Abner on Twitter: https://twitter.com/abnersuarez
- Like us on Facebook: https://www.facebook.com/ForSuchA-TimeAsThisInc
- Keep up to date with our ministry through our e-list and mailing list. Subscribe to both @ www.abnersuarez.com
- Invite Abner to minister at your conference, or church meeting
- Contact us using the information below:

For Such A Time As This, Inc.
PO Box 2461
Dunn, NC 28335
Office: (910) 709-7272
Fax: 1-866-423-1245
E-Mail: info@abnersuarez.com
Web site: www.abnersuarez.com

ADDITIONAL MINISTRY RESOURCES
FROM ABNER SUAREZ

I. ENCOUNTER SCHOOL (6 CD SET)

We live in a historic hour where the first raindrops of the Third Great Awakening and reformation are being poured out in the United States. At the heart of this outpouring are a people who are wholeheartedly living out the greatest commandment (Matthew 22:36-37). **Encounter School is a Six-Part CD Series** designed to equip you through worship, teaching, and impartation to cultivate your personal relationship with G-d. Specific topics and content include:

- G-d's loving kindness toward humanity, even in our weakness and sin

- How are minds can be access points for both heaven and hell

- Ungodly beliefs that destroy the foundation of our relationship with G-d

- Intentionality as a core value in communing with G-d

- Guidance as a byproduct of relationship with G-d

- Experiencing supernatural encounters

- Practical ways to commune with G-d

II. Intimacy Part 1: G-d's Great Invitation to Humanity: (6 CD Set)

The greatest privilege given to humanity was to be created in the image of G-d. This means we're wired for deep, ongoing encounter and communion with G-d. He longs for our lives to be built on the strong foundation of communion with the three Persons of the Trinity. This is the first installment of a five-part series, where Abner examines the biblical characteristics that will help position us as people with lives marked by deep intimacy and friendship with G-d. Specific CD topics include:

- Place Of Divine Encounter
- Victory Through Intimacy
- Living From Identity
- Living From Honor
- Made For Glory
- Mary: A Model Of Encounter

For Such A Time As This, Inc.
PO Box 2461
Dunn, NC 28335
Office: (910) 709-7272
Fax: 1-866-423-1245
E-Mail: info@abnersuarez.com
Web site: www.abnersuarez.com